Contents

KV-197-742

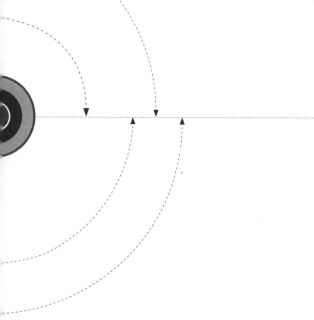

Write on Track

Write on Track

A Guide to Academic Writing

Mary Thoreau

PEARSON
Prentice
Hall

Acknowledgements

Many of the ideas for this book originated while I was teaching academic writing at the Auckland University of Technology. In particular, material in Chapters 8, 10, 14, 18, 19 and 23, and sample essays 1 and 5, have been developed from worksheets and handouts that were produced as part of my employment. While they have since been extensively revised and modified, I would like to thank AUT for the opportunity to include them.

In addition, I would like to thank:

- Philip Thoreau, for his continuing support, inspiration and patience
- Anna Holt, for her encouragement and feedback, which far exceeded the expectations of friendship and collegiality
- Roselle Thoreau, Stan Harrison, Motoko Mori and Shiho Fujisaki for their feedback
- Bronwen Nicholson of Pearson Education for her advice, guidance and encouragement
- Jude Fredricsen of Pearson Education for her painstaking editing
- Kelly Li, for permission to reproduce her essay on pages 279–280
- my students and colleagues, who unknowingly helped me to develop my critical thinking and teaching skills.

Without these people, this book would not have been possible.

Mary Thoreau
June 2005

www.pearsoned.co.nz

Your comments on this book are welcome at
feedback@pearsoned.co.nz

Pearson Education New Zealand
a division of Pearson New Zealand Ltd
Corner Rosedale Road and Airborne Road
Albany, Auckland
New Zealand

Associated companies throughout the world

Produced by Pearson Education New Zealand
Printed in Malaysia, LSP
Typeset in Palatino

We use **paper from sustainable forestry**

SECTION

1

Introduction

This section contains information about this book. It explains what it is about and how it is organised. It also gives suggestions about how you can develop your writing skills.

Chapter 1   What this book is about

1 What this book is about

Learning outcomes

When you have finished studying this chapter, you should be able to:

1 explain what this book is about and how it is organised;

2 identify whether it will be useful for you;

3 explain the value of writing theory;

4 explain the value of practising your writing;

5 identify ways to develop your writing skills.

This book is about writing essays.

What is an essay?

essay a short piece of writing that explains or discusses a point of view about a subject

An essay is a piece of writing about a particular subject. It often explains or discusses a point of view. It is usually short enough to be read 'in one sitting', so the reader should be able to read it reasonably quickly.

What sort of writing is discussed?

tertiary study learning in a university or polytechnic

This book focusses especially on academic writing. It contains information about developing thinking and writing skills for writing essays in preparation for tertiary study in universities and polytechnics. The practical exercises use a mixture of subjects: some academic, some not.

The information in this book is organised for different readers.

Who will find this book useful?

This book is useful for a range of different people.

This book is especially useful for people who want to prepare for tertiary study.

For example, you may be studying in a certificate or foundation course. Perhaps you are studying in Year 12 or Year 13 at high school. Perhaps you left school a while ago. If you are one of these people, you might use the book as a basis for your course.

This book is also useful for people who want to improve their writing skills but are not planning to study.

Although it concentrates on essays, many of the ideas are useful for any sort of writing. In addition, it is organised so that you can use it as a reference, without reading a whole section or chapter.

In addition, the book is suitable for people with different language skills and cultural backgrounds.

You will find the vocabulary easy to understand. Each specialist technical word is explained when it appears for the first time; it is also listed in the glossary at the back of the book. A glossary is a collection of definitions of specialist technical vocabulary. The glossary in this book includes mostly words about writing; it also explains vocabulary that you might find new or difficult.

glossary a collection of definitions of specialist vocabulary

Some information about the words in this book

- This book uses "teacher" to describe any person who is helping someone to learn. Your learning institution might use a different word: "tutor", "lecturer" or "facilitator". If you are studying on your own, your "teacher" might be a friend who is helping you. Only one word is used because it would be confusing and difficult to include all the different ones.
- "S/he" is used for general descriptions of a single person. English does not have an easy way to avoid sexist language. We cannot use "it", because it is suitable only for things and animals. "They" is correct for several people, but sometimes an example is about only one person. In addition, it is clumsy to write "he or she", even though you might say that when you are reading.

Checkpoint

Will this book be useful for you? _____ Why? _____

_____

_____

How is the information organised?

The information is organised into three levels: sections, chapters and divisions.

Each section is about a different subject, but they are all about writing.

For example, Section 2 is about writing styles, and Section 3 is about the writing process.

In addition, the last section (the Appendix) contains information that is useful when you are studying different sections.

For example, it contains sample essays for you to examine, and the glossary.

Checkpoint

Look at the different sections in the book. What are they about?

There are several chapters in each section. Each chapter has specific information about one part of the section.

For instance, the first chapter in Section 4 (Planning) is a general overview; the following chapters are more detailed.

The earlier chapters in a section are more general and are often slightly shorter than the later chapters.

Checkpoint

Look at the chapters in the other sections. Do they follow the same pattern as the chapters in Section 4?

The information in each chapter is organised into divisions. Each division begins with a heading that is written as a statement. The sub-headings are written as questions. The writing in each division answers the questions and supports the statement.

Some of the divisions contain information about the theory of writing.

That is, they explain some specialist technical information about writing.

Some of the divisions are more practical.

That is, they tell you what to do and how to do it.

theory of writing specialist technical information about writing

If you want to be a good writer, you need to know about both theory and practice. See the box about the value of writing theory, on page 5.

Checkpoint

Look at this chapter and identify the divisions of information.

The value of writing theory

Writing an essay is a bit like building a house. A builder joins different materials together to make different parts of the house: walls, a roof, doors and windows. S/he uses equipment to do this, for example a hammer, a saw, a screwdriver, nails. A writer joins different pieces of information together to explain ideas in an essay or story. The writer also has equipment, for example words, paragraphs, grammar and essay outlines.

If you are a builder, your job is easier if you have some specialist knowledge about building. You need to know some building theory: the reasons why a house is built in a particular way. You also need to know some specialist technical words: the name of each part of the house and the names of all the equipment that you will need to use.

If you are a writer, your work is easier if you have some specialist knowledge about writing. You should know why different essays have different structures, and how to organise the information in paragraphs. You should also know the specialist technical words for the different parts of an essay and the equipment that you will need to use.

If you are knowledgeable about the theory of writing, you will be a better writer because you will be able to learn and think about writing more easily.

This book is suitable for people with different learning styles.

What are learning styles?

Everyone is different. Just as people have different interests, so they have different learning styles. These are ways that they prefer to understand and remember information. Educational psychologists have discovered that people learn better if they can use their preferred learning style.

learning style the way that a person prefers to understand and remember information

What are the different learning styles? How is this book suitable for people with different learning styles?

Different researchers have suggested different ways of identifying learning styles. However, most agree on four main styles. They are:

- verbal
- visual
- auditory
- kinaesthetic.

verbal learning style a way of understanding and remembering that involves words, often by reading

Verbal learners like to read words. They often learn better if the information is available as a printed handout that they can read. They often like to read their textbooks before their teacher explains something. They are probably the easiest people to satisfy with a book.

This book is very suitable for them because it uses words.

visual learning style a way of understanding and remembering that involves seeing information

Visual learners are people who like to learn by seeing information. They often like to see what something looks like, or watch someone demonstrating a task. Artists usually have a strong visual preference.

The information in this book is organised so that visual learners can find information easily. For instance:

- The theory and the examples are printed differently from the topic sentences of each paragraph. The examples are printed towards the right side of the page.
- There are lots of diagrams and tables to look at.

auditory learning style a way of understanding and remembering that involves listening

Auditory learners like to learn by listening to information. These people like to discuss ideas. They also like their teacher to explain information. For them, handouts and textbooks are useful as a reminder, but not as the main way of learning.

Most of the exercises in this book suggest that you discuss your ideas with a friend.

kinaesthetic learning style a way of understanding and remembering that involves practical activity

Kinaesthetic people like to be active. They prefer practical activities. Therefore they will often understand information better if they have something to *do* as part of their learning.

There are lots of practical exercises for them to do.

Checkpoint

How do *you* prefer to learn? _____

_____

There are five different sorts of exercise.

How are the exercises organised?

Many of the exercises can be done with other people, in pairs or small groups. However, you should also make sure that you do some of them on your own so that you develop your writing and thinking skills. See the box about the value of practice, on page 7.

The **checkpoint** exercises will help you to develop your thinking and reading skills.

You should do each checkpoint before reading the next paragraph. Use them to think about what you have read.

For example, you have already seen five checkpoints in this chapter. If you did each one thoroughly, you will have a good understanding about how this book is organised.

Checkpoints are quite short. Most of them should take about two minutes to do; none should take more than five minutes. You can usually do them alone, although you may wish to discuss them with a friend.

The **activities** often involve practical writing tasks. The suggested times are guidelines only.

Some people will need longer and some will need less time.

Activities are often linked with checkpoints, but they usually ask you to discuss your answers with someone else.

You will find a **summarising** exercise near the end of every chapter. They are useful for making notes, and to help you think about what you have read. You can do them alone or with other people.

You can **check your understanding** by doing the quizzes about the theory of writing. The answers to the questions are in the Appendix near the end of the book. You will make more progress if you answer the questions before checking the answers!

Train your mind exercises contain suggestions of things you can do to improve your writing. They are often short activities that you can do at the same time as your other work and study. You should choose whatever activities you think you need. If you work on them regularly, you should make good progress.

The value of practice

Learning to write well is a bit like learning to ride a bike. When you learn to ride a bike, you have to remember a lot of different things. For instance, you have to balance, and hold the handlebars, and pedal, and use the brakes carefully, and think about where you going. When you are learning to write an essay, you have to remember to keep to the subject, and organise the information, and explain clearly, and use correct grammar, and show where you found the information.

You cannot learn to ride a bike by reading about it. You have to practise. As you become more skilful, you do not have to remember each part of what you have to do. Everything begins to fit together automatically, and riding becomes enjoyable. In fact, you can begin to experiment with different riding styles: leaning forward or back, two hands or one hand or none!

Writing is a skill that also needs practice. You need to apply the information that you read, until you can do it easily. You can also spend time trying different styles of writing or using different vocabulary. The more skilled you become, the more satisfaction and enjoyment you will get from writing.

Before you use this book, it is a good idea to think about your reasons for writing.

Why do people write?

Most people write because they want someone else to read their writing.

Often, they write because they have to. They do not have any choice.

Perhaps they are writing essays as part of a qualification. Perhaps they have to write reports or letters as part of their jobs.

If they have good writing skills, they are more likely to get good marks or do their work better.

Sometimes people write for their own satisfaction.

This means that they do not care whether anyone reads what they have written. In fact, they may prefer to keep their writing private.

For instance, they may write in a diary.

If they have good writing skills, they will find it easier to record their feelings and ideas.

Some people like to use writing to improve their thinking skills.

Writing is one way to develop their ideas and form opinions. They think carefully about what they write and often re-write several times until they have explained their ideas clearly.

They may write many drafts of an essay before they are satisfied with the final copy.

For these people, good writing skills are important to help them to think clearly.

ACTIVITY 1.1   **Identify your reasons for writing.**

Time suggested:
5 minutes

Why do you want to write?

Tick or cross the boxes in the table and add comments.
When you have finished, discuss with a friend.

Reason for writing	✔ or ✘	Comments
I want someone else to read my writing.		
I have to write.		
I want to write for my own satisfaction.		
I want to use writing to improve my thinking skills.		

You can use this book in different ways.

How can you use this book?

The way that you use this book will depend on your needs.

- You can study each section or chapter separately. This is useful if you are using it as part of an organised writing course. However, you should remember that all the information is related (linked together). If you are reading a general chapter, you will sometimes need to refer to other sections or chapters for detailed information.

- You can use several chapters at the same time. For instance, you may need to look at Chapter 8 (Developing an outline for a simple expository essay) at the same time as you are studying Chapter 22 (Checking content and structure).

- You can use the statements and questions to find specific information, without reading a whole section or chapter. This is useful if you want to check something while you are writing.

- You can choose to read the theory and the examples together, or you can read only the theory, or only the examples. This is useful when you are revising information, or checking it for a special purpose.

Checkpoint

How will you use this book? Will you use one way, or several? Why? _____

_____

_____

While this book provides useful information, you should also work by yourself to develop your writing skills.

What can you do to improve your writing skills?

Firstly, you should read often, and read different sorts of writing.

Reading widely will help you to develop a 'feel' for language, and will improve your grammar and vocabulary. It will also help you to develop a wide general knowledge.

Read fiction and non-fiction; 'light' topics and more serious information; newspapers, magazines and comics; the information on cereal packets as well as the information in encyclopaedias.

Read also *about* writing, so that you develop an understanding of the basic principles of effective writing.

critical thinking careful examination of something; involves thinking about how something is organised and evaluating its quality

Secondly, you should think critically about what you read. This means that you should examine it carefully and think about how it is written and organised. This will help you to evaluate its quality, that is, to decide whether or not it is effective. You should also think about the reasons for your opinions about what you read.

You should also talk about writing.

You can do this in lots of different ways.

- Take part in class discussions.
- Spend time outside of class talking about writing. You could form a study group and make it a part of your regular timetable.
- Exchange essays with other students and give each other feedback.
- Talk about writing with your friends and family if they are happy to help.

In addition, you should spend time thinking about your strengths and weaknesses.

Identify what you are good at, and what you need to improve. Everyone has different skills.

For example:
- One person may be good at spelling, but needs to develop organisation skills.
- Another person may be a clear thinker but has difficulty with grammar. These two people have very different learning needs. The good speller does not need to learn about spelling; s/he should concentrate on how to organise information. The clear thinker needs to work on improving his or her English.

Finally, you need to write. The more you write, the easier it will become. Ideally, you should write every day, even if it is only for a short time. As you write, try to apply the ideas that you learn in class sessions and from your reading and discussions.

Checkpoint

What are your writing strengths? _____

_____

What do you need to improve? _____

_____

What will you do to improve your writing skills? _____

_____

Train your mind

1 Read often.
2 Read different sorts of writing.
3 Think about what you read and whether it is effective or not.
4 Talk about writing.
5 Make a writing study group and meet regularly.
6 Spend time thinking about your writing strengths and weaknesses. Work on your weaknesses.
7 Write something every day.
8 When you write, use the ideas that you have learnt about.

Summarise the chapter

An essay is …	
Organisation of information	**For different readers** • • **For different learning styles** • • • •
Five sorts of exercise	• • • • •
Three reasons for writing	• • •
Working alone to develop writing skills	• • • • •
It is useful to know about writing theory because …	

It is important to practise writing because ...

► Check your understanding ○

Choose the correct answers.
Check whether they are correct (page 286).
If they are not correct, read the information in this chapter again.

1 An essay is:
   a a piece of writing that is used to complete a tertiary assignment
   b a short piece of writing which explains a point of view about a subject
   c a short piece of writing that the reader must examine carefully.

2 The information in this book is suitable for:
   a tertiary study
   b only people who are studying in high school
   c people who want to prepare for tertiary study.

3 You must read all the information in this book in the order that it appears.
   True or false?

4 People can use different ways of learning, but they learn best if they use
   their preferred learning style. True or false?

5 You must complete every exercise if you want to make progress. True or false?

6 The *Checkpoint* exercises:
   a should always be discussed with a friend
   b are designed to help you develop your thinking skills
   c should be done all together when you have finished reading the chapter.

7 You should always do the *Train your mind* exercises with your friends.
   True or false?

8 You should never work with other people when you are thinking about
   writing. True or false?

9 You should know about writing theory because:
   a you will have to join different pieces of information together so you
      should know what words to use
   b the specialist technical words will make you sound knowledgeable, so
      your friends will think you are clever
   c this knowledge will help you to think and talk about writing, so it will
      be easier to improve your writing skills.

10 If you want to improve your writing, you should:
   a write every day
   b write once a week
   c write every time your teacher tells you to.

SECTION

2

Writing styles

This section discusses different writing genres (styles). It also explains the characteristics and general organisation of different academic essays.

Chapter 2   **Genres**

Chapter 3   **Academic essays**

2 Genres

Learning outcomes

When you have finished studying this chapter, you should be able to:

1 explain why good writers use different writing styles for different purposes and different readers;

2 explain some of the characteristics of different writing genres.

Different writing styles are suitable for different target readers.

What is writing style?

"Writing style" describes how something is written.

It involves the words that are used and the way that the information is organised. Different writing styles are suitable for different readers and different purposes.

For example:
- Simple words and short sentences are best for young children.
- Technical words and diagrams are suitable for specialists like engineers.
- Formal English is usually used in business letters.

Good writers choose a writing style that is suitable for their target readers and their writing purpose.

writing style how something is written; the words that are used and the way that the information is organised

What is a target reader?

A target reader is the person who is most likely to read a particular piece of writing. Good writers think about their target readers. They try to write in a way that their target readers will understand and enjoy. Different readers have different needs, skills and preferences.

target reader the person who is most likely to read a specific piece of writing

Checkpoint

Who is the target reader for the writing that *you* will do? _____

_____

What are the differences between different readers?

Different readers have different knowledge and understanding.

Some of these differences are because of age.

Children usually have less knowledge than teenagers; teenagers often have less knowledge than adults.

Some of these differences happen because of differences in education and life experience. Sometimes people's life experiences help them to develop more knowledge and understanding. The more they know already, the easier they find it to learn and understand new ideas.

For example, people who live near the sea have usually spent time walking along the beach. They have often picked up shells or looked carefully at the shrimps and crabs in the rock pools. Therefore, they find it easier to understand information about the creatures who live in the sea.

However, people who have not had lots of different experiences often find it more difficult to gain knowledge.

For instance, people without any scientific knowledge are likely to find it difficult to understand information about DNA.

Therefore, good writers think about their readers' knowledge and understanding. They try to present their ideas in ways that their readers can understand.

Checkpoint

How do *your* knowledge and understanding affect what you read? _____

_____

_____

How do your target reader's knowledge and understanding affect what you write? _____

_____

_____

Different readers are interested in different topics.

They usually prefer to read about subjects that they are interested in. Sometimes their interests are related to their culture, their age, or whether they are male or female. However, people of the same age or the same culture often have different interests.

For example:
- People who enjoy sport are likely to be interested in reading about their preferred sport.
- People who like music are more likely to enjoy reading about it.

Good writers think about what their readers are interested in.

Checkpoint

How do *your* interests affect what you read? _____

_____

How will your target reader's interests affect what you write? _____

_____

_____

Different people have different reading levels.

Some people have advanced reading skills while others need simpler words.

Generally, children are still learning to read, so they prefer short words and sentences. In addition, reading in your first language is easier than reading in a foreign language. People who read a lot often read better than people who do not.

Good writers think about their readers' reading skills. They use words and sentences that their readers are likely to understand.

Checkpoint

How do *your* reading skills affect what you read? _____

_____

_____

How will your target reader's skills affect what you write? _____

_____

_____

Some readers are voluntary, some are 'captives'.

voluntary reader a person who can choose whether to read a particular piece of writing

Voluntary readers can choose to read. While they may want to learn information, they can stop reading if they want to. They do not have to understand all the details.

Readers of magazines, newspapers and popular books are usually voluntary readers.

captive reader a person who must read a particular piece of writing

On the other hand, **captive readers** have little choice. They must read because it is part of their study or work. Often, they must understand the main points and the details.

They may be students reading a textbook or business people reading a report. They may be teachers marking students' essays.

Writing for voluntary readers must be so interesting that the readers do not want to stop. However, good writers should also take care when writing for captive readers. This is because an interested reader will be more willing to continue reading and will remember more of what s/he has read.

Checkpoint

Are *you* a captive or a voluntary reader? How does this affect your reading? _____

_____

_____

_____

To summarise, good writers think carefully about their target readers. They use vocabulary and grammar that their readers will understand. They choose topics and examples that their readers are likely to be interested in. They use a writing style that makes their readers want to keep reading.

ACTIVITY 2.1   **Identify reading preferences and needs.**

Time suggested:
20–30 minutes

Look at your answers for the five *Checkpoints* above.

Part 1 1 Think about what you like to read and what you actually read.
Are they the same or different? Why?

2 Complete the first table.

Part 2 3 What are your target reader's preferences and needs?

4 How will they affect the way that you write?

5 Complete the second table.

6 Discuss your answers with a friend.

What you like to read	What you actually read	Reasons for similarities/ differences
(example) detective stories	*children's stories*	*I read a story to my little sister every evening.*

My target reader is	
Knowledge and understanding	
Interests	

Reading skills	
Captive/voluntary	

These preferences and needs will affect my writing in the following ways:

Different writing styles are suitable for different purposes.

What are the different writing purposes?

There are three main reasons for writing: informing, persuading and entertaining the reader.

- **Informing** is about giving the reader knowledge (or information).
- **Persuading** is about encouraging the reader to accept an idea. The writer presents an opinion or point of view, and shows the reader why s/he should agree with it.
- **Entertaining** is about making the reader interested in a subject.

Sometimes a writer has more than one purpose.

For example, s/he may want to inform and entertain, or inform and persuade, at the same time.

Many people believe that people learn better if they are entertained.

How does purpose affect writing style?

If you want to inform, you must explain all the information that the target reader needs to know. Usually, you should not include information that the reader will think is basic or obvious. So, you should understand what your target reader is likely to know already. However, sometimes you might wish to include important information that the reader already knows. If you are writing an assignment that will be marked, your teacher needs to know how much you understand. Therefore, you should include basic information that s/he already knows.

informing giving someone knowledge or information

Persuading is more complicated than informing because you must try to convince your reader that your opinion is reasonable and correct. Of course, you will probably need to include some factual information. However, your main concern is to encourage your reader to agree with you. Therefore you must present your point of view and give reasons for your opinion.

persuading encouraging someone to accept an idea

Entertaining is about keeping the reader interested. It is not always necessary to make the reader laugh. However, it is important to keep the reader's attention so it must be interesting.

entertaining making someone interested in a subject

Whether you aim to inform, persuade or entertain, you must explain clearly.

vocabulary the words that you use

- You must use words (vocabulary) that most of your target readers can understand.
- You must arrange the words correctly so that they make sense (grammar).

grammar arrangement of words correctly, so that they make sense

- You must include correct and useful information and ideas (content) and organise them logically.

content the information and ideas that are included in an essay

If you do these things, your writing will achieve its purpose.

Checkpoint

What is the purpose (or purposes) of the writing that *you* will do? _____

_____

_____

Different writing styles are suitable for different writing genres.

What is a genre?

When we talk about writing, we use "genre" to describe different kinds (or categories) of writing.

Each genre has a specific writing style that is suitable for the target readers and the writing purpose(s).

genre a category of writing that has a specific writing style

For instance, newspaper writing is different from children's fiction; a thriller story is different from a biography; a recipe is different from a sports article.

Good writers identify the genre that they are working in and use the most suitable writing style for that genre.

ACTIVITY 2.2

Time suggested:
40 minutes

Examine different writing genres.

1   Look at different examples of writing. Choose at least four different genres.
    You could choose:
    - an article in a magazine
    - an article in a newspaper
    - a chapter in a textbook
    - a chapter in a popular book (fiction or non-fiction)
    - an entry in an encyclopaedia
    - a children's book
    - some entries in a dictionary
    - a government or business report.

2   Use the table below to make a list of the differences and similarities.

	Example 1	Example 2	Example 3	Example 4
Who are the target readers?				
Are the target readers captive or voluntary?				
How is the writing style suitable for the target readers?				
What is the writing purpose(s)?				
How is the writing style suitable for the writing purpose(s)?				

3   Discuss your list with a friend.
    - How are the examples different? _____

      _____

    - Are there any similarities? If so, what are they? _____

      _____

      _____

Academic writing is a genre with a special writing style.

What are the characteristics of academic writing?

"Academic writing" describes the sort of writing that is used in polytechnics and universities. Teachers set writing assignments because they want to discover what the students understand about a subject. They often ask the students to give opinions and explain the reasons for those points of view. This is because they want the students to develop thinking skills. Sometimes the ideas and reasons are just as important as the facts.

Usually, the main purpose of academic writing is to inform.

- Students usually write because they want to get good marks and gain a qualification. Therefore they must show their knowledge.
- Some academic writers want to report about their research. They must explain what they have discovered so that their readers can easily understand.

Whether they are students or researchers, they must explain the reasons for their ideas and opinions. This means that they often need to support their ideas with information about other people's research and writing.

Checkpoint

Think about the academic writing that *you* must do.

What is its purpose? _____

_____

_____

Do you need to support your ideas by referring to other writers' work? _____

_____

The target readers are often knowledgeable.

Sometimes they know more about the topic than the writer does. This means that the writer may not need to explain very basic information.

For example, readers who are computer experts will understand specialist words like "modem", "interface" and "bps".

However, if the writer's purpose is to display his or her knowledge, s/he should explain basic information even if it seems obvious.

Checkpoint

Think about the academic writing that *you* will do.

How much basic information should you explain? _____

_____

_____

The target readers are usually captive. That is, they cannot choose whether to stop reading.

- For students, the target reader is usually a teacher or lecturer who will mark their work. Students who write in a clear and well-organised way are more likely to get high marks.
- At postgraduate level, the target readers may be other researchers who are interested in the same topic. They may also need the information to help them with their own research. Researchers who write well will gain respect from other researchers.

Checkpoint

Think about the academic writing that *you* will do.

Who is the target reader? Is there more than one? _____

_____

_____

_____

Academic writing uses a formal writing style.

Usually, academic writers do not refer to themselves in their writing.

That is, they do not use the word "I".

In addition, they avoid slang and casual expressions.

For instance, they use "alright" instead of "OK", and "upset" instead of "hacked off".

They also avoid contractions.

They replace "don't" or "shouldn't" or "they're" with complete words ("do not", "should not", "they are").

In addition, they explain any technical vocabulary that their readers need to understand. Grammar, spelling and punctuation should be 100% correct.

Checkpoint

Think about writing in an academic writing style.

What are *your* writing strengths? _____

_____

_____

What do you need to improve? _____

_____

_____

_____

In conclusion, academic writing is a special writing genre. It aims to inform captive readers who are often already knowledgeable. It uses formal language. Sometimes it involves displaying knowledge that the reader already knows. It must be especially clear and well organised. Students who develop good academic writing skills are more likely to succeed in tertiary study.

ACTIVITY 2.3

Time suggested:
15–20 minutes

Compare academic writing with other genres.

1 Choose two of the writing genres that you examined in Activity 2.2.
2 Compare them with academic writing.
3 Use the table below for your notes.
4 Discuss your answers with a friend.

	Academic writing	Genre 1	Genre 2
Purpose(s)			
Target reader(s)			
Writing style			

Train your mind

1 Read different sorts of writing and think about the differences between the genres.
2 When you write, think about the needs and preferences of your target reader(s).
3 When you read or hear information, think about whether the writer (or speaker) is trying to inform, persuade or entertain.
4 Identify the purpose(s) of your essay before you start to write.
5 When you read or hear casual language, practise turning it into a formal style.

Summarise the chapter

Reasons for using different writing styles	• Target reader(s) • Purpose(s)
A genre is … For example …	
Different target readers	1 2 3 4
Writing purposes	• Informing • Persuading • Entertaining

Important to explain clearly	• Vocabulary • Grammar • Content
Academic writing	• Purpose • Target reader(s) • Writing style

► Check your understanding ○

Choose the correct answers.
Check whether they are correct (page 286).
If they are not correct, read the information in this chapter again.

1 When you write, your target reader is:
   a a person who has the same ideas as you have
   b the sort of person who is most likely to read your writing
   c the sort of person who is most likely to disagree with you.

2 Good writers choose the style of writing that they find easiest. True or false?

3 Different readers have:
   a different knowledge and understanding
   b different hobbies and interests
   c different levels of reading
   d all of the above.

4 If you write an essay in an examination, the person who marks the essay is:
   a a captive reader
   b a voluntary reader
   c a reluctant reader.

5 When you write persuasively, you want your reader to agree with your ideas. True or false?

6 A writing genre is:
   a a category of writing that is suitable for newspaper readers
   b a category of writing about a general subject
   c a category of writing that has a specific writing style.

7 Good writing skills are useful for students because:
   a they want to entertain their teachers
   b they want to show how much they know
   c they want to do some research.

8 When you write an academic essay, your target reader often knows about the subject already. True or false?

9   "Content" is a technical word that describes:
  a   the information and ideas that are included in an essay
  b   the words that you use in an essay
  c   the grammar that you use in an essay.

10 Academic writing uses:
  a   casual language
  b   foreign language
  c   formal language.

3 Academic essays

Learning outcomes

When you have finished studying this chapter, you should be able to:

1. explain the characteristics of three different genres of academic essay;
2. outline the general structure of each genre.

Each genre (type) of academic essay has a different purpose.

What are the different academic essay genres and what are their purposes?

If you know about two essay genres, you will have a good foundation for tertiary study.

- Expository essays explain.
  - The most simple expository essays explain about one subject or idea.
  - Comparative expository essays explain two or more subjects or ideas, and identify similarities and differences.
- Argumentative essays aim to persuade their readers to agree with a point of view (or opinion). Sometimes they are called persuasive essays.

It is important to remember that this sort of division is a generalisation. This means that it is usually, but not always, true. Really, the different genres have many similarities as well as differences.

expository essay writing that explains

simple expository essay writing that explains about one subject or idea

comparative expository essay writing that explains two or more subjects or ideas, and identifies similarities and differences

argumentative essay writing that aims to persuade the reader to agree with a point of view

generalisation a statement that is usually, but not always, true

---

Checkpoint

What sort of information would you expect to find in each type of essay? _____

_____

_____

_____

While they have differences, the essay genres overlap to make a continuum.

What are their differences?

The main difference between expository and argumentative writing is whether or not the writer is trying to persuade the reader.

Therefore, they are organised in different ways, and they use different language.

Suppose that you were writing an expository essay about the interesting places for tourists to visit in Bangkok.

- In a simple expository essay, you would describe the different places and explain why they are interesting.
- In a comparative expository essay, you would describe and explain examples from Bangkok and another city. You would also discuss any similarities and differences.
- In an argumentative essay, you might try to persuade the reader that s/he should visit Bangkok.

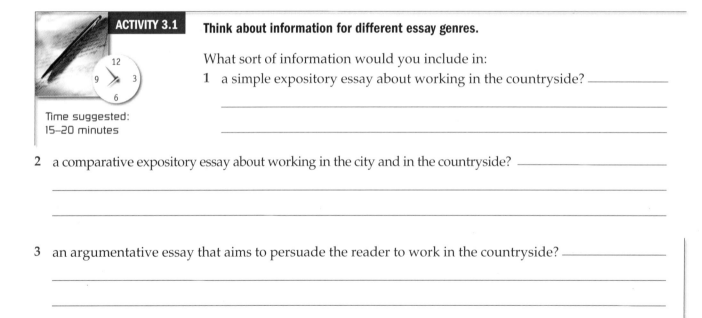

ACTIVITY 3.1

Time suggested:
15–20 minutes

Think about information for different essay genres.

What sort of information would you include in:

1 a simple expository essay about working in the countryside? _____

_____

_____

2 a comparative expository essay about working in the city and in the countryside? _____

_____

_____

3 an argumentative essay that aims to persuade the reader to work in the countryside? _____

_____

_____

When you have finished, discuss your answers with a friend.

How do the different essay genres overlap?

overlap when different things share some of the same characteristics

Overlap happens when different things share some of the same characteristics. We can use a circle diagram to show how two different things are similar and different.

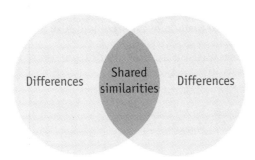

Figure 3.1   A circle diagram showing overlap

If we compare expository and argumentative essays, we can find some similarities as well as differences.

Both argumentative and expository essays can contain your ideas and opinions.

> Your teachers usually want more than just facts. They want you to show that you have thought about a subject and have developed a point of view. Therefore, you will usually include some opinions in both sorts of essay.

> In the essay example about Bangkok, your teacher would expect you to state that Bangkok is an interesting place. This is an opinion, because other people might disagree.

Both expository and argumentative essays can contain some factual information.

> Your teachers want you to justify your ideas. That is, they want you to explain the reasons for your opinions and statements. You can do this by explaining some factual information.

> In the Bangkok essay, you would justify your opinions with facts about the places you describe. You might also include some general background information, like where Bangkok is and how long it would take to get there.

justify explain the reasons for your ideas or statements

ACTIVITY 3.2

Time suggested:
5–10 minutes

Think of opinions to include in an expository essay.

1 Imagine that you were writing an expository essay about living in the countryside.

2 What opinions would you include?

_____

_____

_____

3 Discuss your answers with a friend.

ACTIVITY 3.3

Time suggested:
5–10 minutes

Think of factual information to include in an argumentative essay.

1 Imagine that you were writing an argumentative essay to persuade your reader to live in the countryside.

2 What factual information would you include?

_____

_____

_____

3 Discuss your answers with a friend.

Checkpoint

How could you use circles to show how expository and argumentative essays overlap? Draw a diagram.

continuum a line diagram that shows how different types of something are related

How do the different essay genres make a continuum?

We could use a line diagram to show how things overlap. This sort of diagram is called a continuum. It is very useful to show how different types of something are related. In this case, we can show the different sorts of essay.

| expository writing | only facts, no opinions | mostly facts, some opinions | equal mixture of facts and opinions | some facts, mostly opinions | few or no facts, all opinions | argumentative writing |

Figure 3.2 A continuum showing different essay genres

Most of your academic writing will probably be near the middle of the continuum.

Checkpoint

Think about the last essay you wrote (or the one that you are writing now). Use a cross to show where it belongs on the continuum below.

only facts,
no opinions

few or no
facts, almost
all opinions

Although they have some similarities, the different essay genres have different structures.

What is structure?

"Structure" describes the way that something is organised. When you are writing an essay, you want the reader to understand your message, that is, your explanation and ideas about a subject. Therefore, you must organise the essay so that the reader can understand it easily.

structure the way that something is organised

What are the similarities?

You must organise every essay so that it has an introduction, a body and a conclusion.

- The **introduction** is placed at the beginning of the essay. It tells the reader what the essay is about.
- The **body** follows the introduction. It contains the information and ideas that the writer wants the reader to understand.
- The **conclusion** is placed at the end of the essay. It shows the reader how the content in the body supports the main message of the essay.

People use this structure for a lot of their communication with each other.

For example, most telephone and face-to-face conversations, and most letters, have a beginning, a middle and an end.

If one part is missing, the structure will be incomplete. Then the reader or listener will find it difficult to understand what the writer or speaker wants to say.

Checkpoint

Think of a letter you received, or a conversation that you had, where the structure was incomplete.

Which part was missing? _____

What problems did you have with understanding the message? _____

_____

What are the different structures?

An **expository essay** usually follows a simple structure.

- The introduction usually contains some general information, as well as the subject and the writer's point of view.

- The body contains information that explains the subject. It often gives reasons for the writer's point of view. It is important to arrange the information in the body in a logical order. This means that it is organised so that the reader can understand it easily. You must take extra care with a comparative essay, because the information is more complicated.

- The conclusion repeats the subject and opinion.

This is a very brief explanation. There is more detailed information about organising expository essays in Chapter 8 (pages 79–87) and Chapter 9 (88–95).

logical order arranged so that the reader can understand the information easily

---

Checkpoint

Why is the information in a comparative essay more complicated than in a simple expository essay?

_____

_____

An **argumentative essay** often uses a more complicated structure than an expository one does.

- The introduction must tell the reader the subject of the essay. It may also include the writer's opinion. However, if the target reader is likely to disagree strongly, the writer may decide to leave the opinion until later in the essay.

- The body is often organised into a classical structure.
    - It starts by presenting and explaining the writer's opinions (confirmation).
    - It then presents and explains some of the opposite opinions (concession).
    - It then tries to persuade the reader that the opposite opinions are not correct or reasonable (refutation).

- The conclusion persuades the reader to accept the writer's point of view. If the writer's opinion was not included in the introduction, it is often placed here.

Again, this description is very brief. You can read more about argumentative essay structure in Chapter 10 (pages 96–106).

classical structure organisation of an argumentative essay that uses confirmation, concession and refutation

---

Checkpoint

Why is an argumentative essay more complicated than an expository essay? _____

_____

_____

How do you know which sort of essay to write?

It is very important to read the essay question carefully so that you know what the teacher wants you to do. If you do this, your essay will be on track, and you will get better marks.

You should analyse the essay question. This means that you must examine it and think carefully about what it means. Identify key words that show what you are expected to do. Generally, you should **write an expository essay** if the question includes words like:

> **analyse** examine what you read and think carefully about it

- explain
- define
- outline
- examine
- compare (and contrast).

You should **write an argumentative essay** if the question includes words like:

- argue
- discuss
- evaluate

Chapter 6 contains more information about analysing essay questions. (See pages 60–69.)

Checkpoint

Think of the last essay that you wrote (or the one that you are writing now).

Was it expository or argumentative? How did you know? _____

_____

_____

Train your mind

1 Always analyse essay questions before you begin to write them.
2 When you read, think about whether the writing is expository or argumentative.
3 When you read, identify the structure of the writing.
4 When you are talking to people, think about whether the discussion is expository or argumentative.
5 When you are talking to people, identify the structure of the conversation.

Summarise the chapter

Essay type	Purpose	Structure
Expository	• Simple expository • Comparative expository	
Argumentative		
Some overlap		
Analyse by checking keywords	Expository	
	Argumentative	

► Check your understanding

Choose the correct answers.

Check whether they are correct (page 286).

If they are not correct, read the information in this chapter again.

1 Expository essays are different from argumentative essays because:
   a an expository essay aims to expose and an argumentative essay aims to persuade
   b an expository essay aims to explain and an argumentative essay aims to persuade
   c an expository essay aims to explain and an argumentative essay aims to disagree.

2 A comparative essay looks at how two or more things are the same, and how they are different. True or false?

3 Different essay genres overlap because:
   a they can both contain ideas and opinions
   b they can both explain factual information
   c they can both contain explanations and opinions.

4 A continuum is a set of circles. True or false?

5 Structure is about:
   a how something is organised
   b being strict and serious
   c how things are different and similar.

6 An essay is different from a spoken discussion because it contains a beginning, a middle and an end. True or false?

7 You should use a classical structure for:
   a an expository essay
   b a comparative essay
   c an argumentative essay.

8 A classical structure contains only information about the writer's opinions. True or false?

9 The introduction must always include the writer's opinion. True or false?

10 If you analyse the essay question, you are more likely to understand what the teacher wants you to do. True or false?

The writing process

This section discusses how to organise the way that you write. It examines five different actions that you must take when you write an essay. It also gives suggestions about writing with other people.

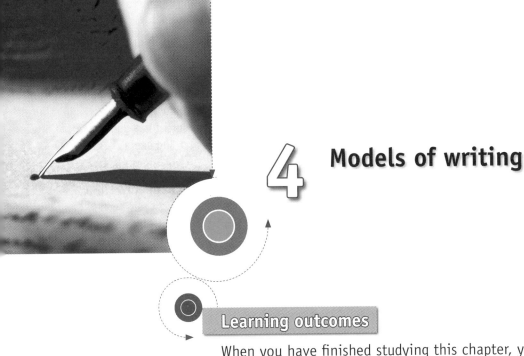

4 Models of writing

You will write better if you know about writing processes.

What are writing processes?

A process is a way of doing something. When we talk about writing processes, we mean the actions that people take when they plan and complete a writing task. This includes the order that the actions happen in. Good writers think about how to organise the writing process. The way that they do this depends on their preferred style and the writing task that they are working on. Therefore, it is useful to know about different writing processes.

> **writing processes** the actions that people take when they plan and complete a writing task; the order that the actions happen in

How can knowing about writing processes help you to write better?

You can produce a better essay and save a lot of time if you know some theory and principles about writing.

> **theory and principles** the 'rules' and ideas that people have developed about a particular subject

That is, you need to know the 'rules' and ideas that people have developed about writing. This is true of many activities, not just writing.

For example, suppose that you want to make a special cake but you are not an expert cook. You can make a good cake more quickly if you use a recipe that someone else has written or told you about. It would also be cheaper, because you would not waste ingredients.

Most students do not want to waste time because they have to complete assignments quickly, and they want to get good results. Therefore it is a good idea to know about the writing processes that other people use and find useful.

Knowing about the writing process will also help you to plan your time.

Writing is often a slow activity. It needs a lot of thinking and often a lot of re-writing.

For instance, each chapter in this book had at least five drafts before it was sent to the publisher. In addition, it was revised several more times before it was printed.

You probably know people who write their essays just before they are due, and get good marks.

They say things like, "I didn't spend a lot of time on it. I just wrote it the night before. I can't believe I got a B+."

However, these people forget about the amount of time they spent thinking about the subject before they began writing. They would get even better marks if they spent as much time on writing as on thinking.

Understanding the stages of writing will help you find solutions when you have a specific problem.

Every writer has difficulties sometimes. Writing problems are often a sign that a particular stage of the writing process needs more work.

For example:
- If you cannot think what to write, it may be because you do not have enough information. Therefore you need to do more research.
- If you cannot decide the order of the paragraphs, it may be because you do not have a deep enough understanding. Therefore you need to do more thinking.

In addition, understanding the writing process can help you decide how to improve your skills. You will find it easier to understand what you are good at and where you need to improve.

For example, suppose that you find it difficult to explain what you mean. It may be because you have poor research skills, or it may be because you need to improve your vocabulary.

As a result, you can concentrate on your weakest areas and plan how to overcome them.

Should you always follow a writing process?

The more organised you are, the more marks you are likely to get. Generally, your teachers want you to show that you have thought about a subject and that you understand it. If you follow a writing process, your work will be well researched and more thoughtful.

This does not mean that you should always work in the same way, or in the same way as everyone else. Instead, you should think about the needs of each writing task, and your own working and learning preferences. So, although you should follow the stages of a writing process, you must choose a way of doing this that suits you and the job that you are doing.

For example:
- You must decide how much planning to do.
- You must think about how much to research.
- You must think about the order of the actions that you will take when you write.

Checkpoint

How do you usually organise your writing? Can you identify a pattern of behaviour? _____

_____

_____

_____

We can use models to describe the writing process.

What are models?

A model is a way of describing a process. It can use words or a diagram or both. Writing process models use words and diagrams to explain how people organise their writing.

    There are several models of the writing process. Their differences are mainly about the number of stages. We will use a five-stage model because it is clear and easy to remember. The five stages in the model are:

model a way of describing a process, often using words and diagrams

1 planning
2 researching
3 writing
4 editing
5 proof-reading.

You can use a mnemonic to remember the five stages.

mnemonic a group of letters or words that you can use to help you remember something

A mnemonic (pronounced 'ne-mon-ik') is a group of letters or words that you can use to help you remember something.

For example, many primary school children use "Never Eat Soggy Weet-Bix" to help them learn the points of the compass (North, East, South, West).

If the words are funny or silly you are more likely to remember them.

You could use '**P**rofessors **R**arely **W**rite **E**verything **P**erfectly' to remind you of the first letter of each stage of the writing process. If you wish, you could make up your own mnemonic to have a personal reminder.

Checkpoint

Make up your own mnemonic to help you remember the five stages of writing. _____

_____

planning the stage when the writer considers how to organise the essay

outline a list of the information that will be included in an essay, and the order that it will be presented in

What happens at each stage of the writing process?

At the **planning** stage, you should consider the essay question and prepare an outline. The outline contains the information that will be included in the essay, and the order that it will be presented in. An outline is often written in note form (not sentences), because the ideas are more important than the words that will be used. It is a good idea to identify similar ideas so that they can be grouped together.

Checkpoint

Think about the last essay that you wrote .

How much time did you spend on the planning stage?

What did your outline look like? _____

_____

_____

researching the stage of the writing process when you find information

The **research** stage is about finding information. You must identify what information you already know. Then you must decide what research is needed and how to do it. This usually involves reading or talking to people. However, sometimes it is useful to watch a television programme or a video, or listen to a radio programme. If the information is complicated, it is a good idea to make notes as the research is being done.

Checkpoint

Think about the last essay that you wrote.

How much research did you need to do?

What sort of information did you need to find? _____

_____

_____

At the **writing** stage you produce a first draft of your essay. This is when the writing begins to look like an essay. You should look at all the information you have collected and decide what is relevant. That is, you must think about whether the information is about the subject of your essay and whether it would be useful to include it. Then use sentences to develop the outline.

> **writing** the stage of the writing process when you select information and use sentences to develop the outline
>
> **relevant** about the subject that you are discussing; useful for your essay

Checkpoint

Think about the last essay that you wrote.

How many drafts did you write?

What did your first draft look like? _____

_____

_____

During the **editing** stage, you make sure that the content (information in the essay) is complete, relevant and well organised. If there is any information missing, then you may have to do more research. You must delete information that is not relevant or useful. When the paragraphs have been arranged into a logical order, the second draft is completed. Now you are ready for the final stage.

> **editing** the stage of the writing process when you make sure that the content is complete, relevant and well organised

Checkpoint

Think about the last essay that you wrote.

How much time did you spend on the editing stage?

What sort of changes did you make? _____

_____

_____

proof-reading checking that grammar, spelling and punctuation are correct

The final stage is **proof-reading**. This is when the essay is 'polished'. You make sure that all grammar, spelling and punctuation are correct. In addition, you should check the presentation. For instance, the essay may need to be double spaced; or a cover sheet may be required. When you have completed this stage, your final copy is ready to be handed in.

Checkpoint

Think about the last essay that you wrote.

How much time did you spend on the proof-reading stage?

What sort of mistakes did you correct? _____

_____

_____

You should know about two different models of the writing process.

What are the two models?

The two models are:
- the linear model
- the cyclical model.

Both models contain the five stages that we have discussed. However, they use them in different ways.

What is the linear model?

linear model a description of a process where several stages are completed in order

"Linear" means "line", so the linear model is about organising the writing process step by step. This traditional model was developed by writers who used pens or pencils or typewriters to write directly onto paper. They observed that many of them used a similar writing process, that is, the same pattern of working. Whenever they wanted to change some of the words, they had to erase and replace them, or else re-write a whole page of writing. This was time-consuming and often difficult to organise. Therefore, many writers tried to plan most of their work and finish their research before they began to write. Generally, they used the five stages (listed on page 41) separately and in order (one after the other).

The linear model can be drawn as a diagram, as shown on the right.

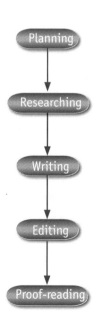

Figure 4.1 Linear model of the writing process

↓*Checkpoint*

Think about how you could use the linear model for your own writing (or think about a time when you did use it).

What advantages can you think of? _____

_____

_____

What are the disadvantages? _____

_____

_____

What is the cyclical model?

The cyclical model uses the same stages as the linear model but it is more flexible.

> **cyclical model** a description of a flexible process in which the order of the stages can be changed or repeated

It describes how many people write when they use computers. "Cyclical" means that the stages happen in circles, rather like the movement of a bicycle wheel. You can move easily between the stages, and can repeat stages if you need to.

For instance, you can think of new ideas (plan), research them and add them to the essay at any time. Computers also make it easy to "cut and paste", so you can change words quickly.

If you look at the diagram below, you can see some of the cycles that can occur.

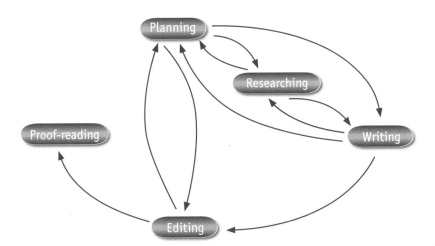

Figure 4.2 Cyclical model of the writing process

Checkpoint

How many circles can you find in the cyclical model? (You should be able to find at least five.)

Why is there no arrow leading away from the proof-reading stage? _____

_____

ACTIVITY 4.1

Time suggested:
5–10 minutes

Think about how you organise the writing process.

1   Think about the way that you write.

2   Do you use a linear or a cyclical model? _____

3   What advantages and disadvantages can you think of, for the model that you use?

- Some advantages: _____

  _____

  _____

- Some advantages: _____

  _____

  _____

4   Discuss your answers with a friend.

Which model should you use?

You should use whichever model you find most useful. Different people often prefer to work in different ways because they have different thinking and learning styles. It may be a good idea to spend time thinking about the way you prefer to think and learn.

The linear model is probably most suitable for people who like to complete each stage before moving to the next one.

If you are this sort of person, you should remember that it is sometimes important to 'back track'.

For instance, if you need more information when you are writing, you may need to return to the research stage.

The cyclical model is probably best for people who like to be flexible.

It is especially useful if you like to use the computer for writing. However, it can be time-consuming.

For instance:
- You may find that you keep doing extra research, even if you already have enough information.
- You may be tempted to spend a lot of time rewriting the content, even though it is already well organised.

Whatever model you use, you should probably work on proof-reading last, after you have finished writing the content.

Train your mind

1 Think about how you prefer to think and learn.
2 When you are writing, think about the stage that you are working on.
3 Talk with others about how they organise their writing.
4 Use your knowledge of the writing process to help you identify your writing problems.
5 Concentrate on improving the things that you find difficult.

Summarise the chapter

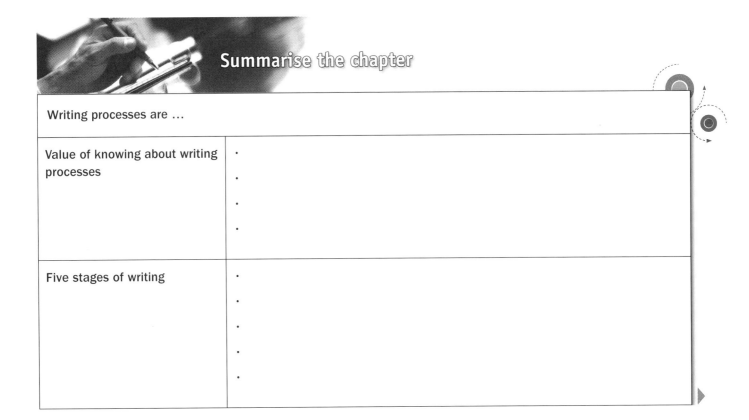

Writing processes are …	
Value of knowing about writing processes	• • • •
Five stages of writing	• • • • •

A model is ...	
Linear model	(Use words to describe)
	(Draw a diagram)
	Most suitable for ...
Cyclical model	(Use words to describe)
	(Draw a diagram)
	Most suitable for ...

► Check your understanding

Choose the correct answers.
Check whether they are correct (page 286).
If they are not correct, read the information in this chapter again.

1　The writing process is:
   a　the actions that you take when you write
   b　the way that the computer organises your writing
   c　the actions that only professional writers use when they write.

2　If you know about writing processes, you will need more time to write. True or false?

3　It is easier to identify your writing problems if you know about the stages of the writing process. True or false?

4　When we are talking about writing processes, a model is:
   a　a person who shows us how to write an essay
   b　a set of essays that we should copy
   c　a way of describing what people do when they write.

5 We can use words and/or diagrams to describe models. True or false?

6 The five stages of the writing process are:
  a planning, researching, proof-reading, copying, correcting
  b researching, editing, planning, writing, organising
  c planning, researching, writing, editing, proof-reading.

7 You must always use the five stages of the writing process in the correct order. True or false?

8 A first draft is:
  a the first time that you make notes for an essay
  b the first time that you write sentences for an essay
  c the first time that your teacher reads your essay.

9 The linear model describes the number of lines that appear on a page when you write. True or false?

10 In the cyclical model:
  a you must follow the stages in order (step by step)
  b you can repeat the stages
  c you must repeat every stage.

5 Writing collaboratively

Learning outcomes

When you have finished studying this chapter, you should be able to:

1 explain the advantages and disadvantages of writing collaboratively;

2 explain some strategies to manage the collaborative writing process.

Collaborative writing needs extra care.

What is collaborative writing?

collaborative writing two or more people working together to produce one piece of work

"Collaboration" happens when people work together to make one product. When writers do this, they produce one piece of work which they have all contributed to. They may do this because they have different specialised knowledge which needs to be combined. Sometimes they may have to work together because of the way that an assignment or project is organised. When people write collaboratively, everyone has to agree. However, different people often have different ideas and different ways of thinking. This makes the writing process more complicated. Collaborative writing is more difficult than writing alone.

Checkpoint

Think about a time when you wrote something with another person.

What were the advantages of collaborating? _____

_____

_____

_____

What were the disadvantages? _____

_____

_____

_____

How should you organise the writing process when you write collaboratively?

You should agree about what everyone will do, before you start to work.

Different methods (ways of working) suit different groups.

For example, there are different ways to organise your research.
- One person can do all the research, then report to the group.
- Two people can do the research together, then report to the rest of the group.
- The research task can be divided between all the group members, then reported at a general group meeting.
- Each person can research only the information that s/he will write about.

Whatever method you use, all the members in the group must agree about it.

method a way of organising a task

ACTIVITY 5.1

Time suggested: 10–15 minutes

Think about how to organise the collaborative writing process.

1 Think about the five stages of the writing process.
   - How could they be organised in a collaborative situation?
   - What are the advantages and disadvantages of each method?
2 Use the table below to make notes. The research stage is given as an example.
3 Discuss your answers with a friend.

Stage	Possible Methods	Advantages and disadvantages
Planning		
Researching *(example)*	1 One person researches, reports to group. 2 Two people research, report to group. 3 Each person researches a bit, reports to group. All use the information. 4 Each person researches only the section that s/he will write (individual research).	1 Possible problems with sharing information 2 Can teach each other 3 Can complete more research 4 Possible problems with sharing information
Writing		

Stage (continued)	Possible Methods (continued)	Advantages and disadvantages (continued)
Content check and second draft		
Proof-reading and final copy		

What methods can you use for the planning stage?

You have probably realised that planning should be done together. It should be done first and reviewed often. The more thoroughly you plan, the easier the rest of the writing task will be.

At the beginning you should:

- Decide what each person will do. This is easier if you know each person's strengths and weaknesses.
- Organise times for meetings. This will allow people to plan their personal lives.
- Exchange contact details, like phone numbers and e-mail addresses.

Later, you must make sure that everything is developing in the way that you want (and the way that you have agreed).

If you are planning with other people, you should allow more time than if you are working alone.

The main advantage of planning together is that you can use lots of different ideas.

The more you discuss your ideas, the more you will learn and the better your essay will be.

However, this can be time-consuming, especially when people disagree. If there are problems with disagreements, you should allow extra time to talk.

What methods can you use for the research stage?

Your research method will depend on the skills of the people in the group.

It is often a good idea to organise tasks so that people can use the skills that they are good at.

For example, one person may have better research skills than the others in the group.

However, if someone needs to develop a skill, that person should take part in a task that will help them to learn it.

Perhaps one person has poor research skills and needs to improve them. S/he could work with (and learn from) someone with good research skills.

It is also important to think about the sort of research that you need to do.

If you need only one piece of information, it is easy for one person to find it.

For example, if you need to find the meaning of a word, it would be a waste of time for everyone to check it in the dictionary.

If the research task is big or complicated, it may be better to share it. It is easier to do this if the task can be divided into different sections.

Suppose that you were writing an essay about genetic engineering. The research could be divided into three small sections:

1 how GE can be used for medical treatment
2 how it can be used for food production
3 the reasons why some people disagree with GE.

A different person could research each section.

Individual research is most suitable if each writer is working on a completely separate section. However, it needs careful organisation if there are strong links between the different sections.

If you research collaboratively, you should allow time to discuss your research. There are two advantages in collaborative research. Perhaps the main one is that several people working together can do more research than one person working alone. In addition, working together can help people to learn a lot. However, it is important to allow enough time for everyone to share and understand the research information.

What methods can you use for the writing stage?

There are two ways to organise the way you write the first draft.

- Each person can write a section alone.
- Alternatively, everyone can work together, perhaps all sitting around the computer.

It is also important to remember that people have different working and learning preferences.

Writing alone is generally quicker than writing together because there is no need for discussion. However, if you write together you can help each other with information and ideas. A well-developed first draft may mean that you spend less time on later stages of the writing process.

◀- -

▾ *Checkpoint*

Suppose that you were writing an essay about genetic engineering.

If you decided that each person would write a section alone, how would you divide the

writing tasks? _____

_____

_____

_____

What methods can you use for the editing stage?

When you edit, you will probably prefer to work together.

> Certainly you should spend time discussing
> the content. If everyone works alone, it is more
> difficult for the group to identify gaps or overlaps.

>> For instance, in the genetic engineering example, you would need to
>> make sure that all the information was included. You would also check
>> that two people had not used the same information.

> On the other hand, working together is often time-
> consuming because you must discuss and reach agreement.

It is important to develop a co-operative attitude.

> Sometimes, it may be difficult to accept what other people
> say about your writing, especially if they want to change it.

>> You may feel as though they are saying that you are not good or clever or
>> sensible. It is easy to become defensive and try to protect your work.

> It is important to remember that your writing is a product.
> It is not part of your personality, so you should not feel
> threatened. Instead you should try to understand why the
> others want to change your words or add to your ideas.

>> You can say something like, "Please explain why you want to change this
>> sentence" or "I'm not sure about your reasons for wanting to make this change."

> It is also important to think carefully about what you will say if you
> want to change someone else's writing. You do not want to hurt
> people's feelings, because you must continue to work with them.
> However, you want to make sure that the piece of writing is the best
> that you can make it. Therefore, it is important to have open and
> honest discussion.

Checkpoint

Suppose that you were writing about genetic engineering.

If you were working with other people, how would you like to organise the editing stage?

_____

_____

_____

What methods can you use for proof-reading?

There are three possible ways to organise this stage.

- You could choose to hold a meeting and proof-read together. While this would be very slow, it would give you a lot of opportunity for discussion. If everyone takes part, you are more likely to do a good job. Again, it is important during the discussion to be considerate about other people's feelings.
- Each person could work alone and then the whole group could meet for discussion. Preparing beforehand is always a good idea because it gives two opportunities to make sure that everything is correct.
- One person could do all the proof-reading. This is alright if the person is good at English and is good at noticing mistakes. However, it can be a problem if s/he is not careful or conscientious.

Checkpoint

Suppose that you were writing an essay about genetic engineering.

If you were working with other people, how would you like to organise the proof-reading?

_____

_____

_____

Train your mind

1 Spend some time identifying your strengths and weaknesses.
2 Agree about how you will divide the work.
3 Make sure that you review your work and its progress regularly.
4 Think about how you like to be treated, and treat the others in your group in the same way.
5 Attend all meetings, and arrive on time.

Summarise the chapter

Collaborative writing is ...	
When you write collaboratively, it is important to agree how to organise the tasks because ...	

Planning	At the beginning · · · Later · · Main advantage: Main disadvantage:
Researching	· · Main advantage: Main disadvantage:
Writing	· · Main advantage: Main disadvantage:
Editing	· Accepting others' comments · Giving feedback Main advantage: Main disadvantage:

Proof-reading	·
	·
	·
	Main advantage:
	Main disadvantage:

► Check your understanding ○

Choose the correct answers.
Check whether they are correct (page 286).
If they are not correct, read the information in this chapter again.

1 Collaborative writing happens when:
   a you copy someone else's writing
   b someone copies your writing
   c you work with other people to write together.

2 Collaborative writing is often more difficult than writing alone because people never agree. True or false?

3 When you begin to work together, you should:
   a hope that everyone works hard
   b decide what everyone will do
   c go out for a meal together.

4 You should know the phone numbers or e-mail addresses of the other people in your group. True or false?

5 When you are researching:
   a the person with the worst research skills should do all the work, so that s/he learns how to research
   b the person with the best research skills should do all the work, so that the research is good
   c you should divide the work, depending on the task that you need to do.

6 When you are writing, everyone should sit around the computer at the same time. True or false?

7 When you are editing, you should make sure that:
   a there are no gaps or overlaps
   b all the spelling is correct
   c the information about genetic engineering is correct.

8 Only one person should do the proof-reading. True or false?

9 When you give or receive feedback:

   a you should remember that your writing is not the same as your personality

   b you should say whatever you think, as long as the essay is the best that you can produce

   c you should not make any suggestions, because you do not want to hurt other people's feelings.

10 Writing collaboratively often takes more time than writing alone. True or false?

SECTION

4

Planning

This chapter discusses how to plan an essay. It examines a model of the planning stage. It also gives suggestions about finding ideas and developing an outline.

6 Beginning to plan

When you have finished studying this chapter, you should be able to:

1 explain why planning is important;
2 explain the planning process;
3 explain how to analyse an essay question.

Planning is an important part of essay writing.

What is planning?

planning the stage when the writer considers how to organise the essay

When you plan, you consider how to organise the essay. You think about:

- what information to include
- what order to present the information in
- what research to do.

Why is planning important?

Planning affects the quality of your essay. If you spend time thinking about the subject, the content of your essay is more likely to be on track. In addition, your ideas will be better developed. Therefore your essay will improve, you will learn more, and you will get better marks. If you fail to plan, you may be planning to fail.

You can use a model of the planning process.

What does the model look like?

There are four stages in the planning process:

- analysis
- finding ideas
- selecting and clustering
- developing an outline.

Checkpoint

Think of a mnemonic to help you remember the stages.

What would you do at each stage? _____

_____

_____

_____

_____

_____

You can choose whether to use the stages in a linear or cyclical way. (See pages 44–47 in Chapter 4 if you need more information about this.) Many writers find that they follow a cyclical process, moving between the different stages several times.

Thinking has not been included as a separate stage in this model because it is an important part of *every* stage. In fact, it is impossible to plan well if you do not spend time thinking carefully.

A cyclical model of the planning process might look like this:

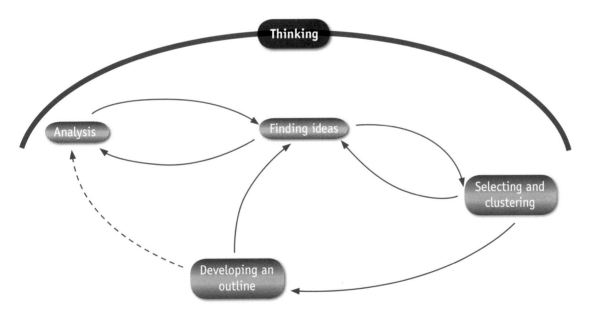

Figure 6.1   Cyclical model of the planning process

Checkpoint

Identify different circles in the diagram of the planning process. You should be able to find four.

How should you plan?

It is usually a good idea to begin with analysis and end with the outline.

However, you can move between the other stages.

For example:
- You will often select and record information while you are researching.
- You may begin to cluster information and ideas as you record them.
- When you are writing the outline, you might decide to do more research.

You should also check that the outline provides a good answer for the essay question; this is shown by the dotted line in Figure 6.1 (page 61).

You should begin by making an analysis.

What is analysis?

analyse examine what you read and think carefully about it

When you analyse something, you examine it and think carefully about how it is made and what it means. Analysis helps you to understand what you have to do.

What (and how) should you analyse?

It is a good idea to **analyse the question**. Think carefully about what it means and what the teacher wants you to do. Essay 'questions' can be presented in several different ways.

Sometimes your teacher will give you a **thesis statement**.

This is a sentence that tells the reader what the essay is about and introduces the writer's point of view. This is often the easiest sort of 'question'. It tells you what point of view you must support and gives some information about what to include.

These examples are all thesis statements.
- A varied diet is an important part of keeping healthy.
- Globalisation has had far-reaching effects on the development of our society.
- The bicycle is a good form of transport.

There is more information about thesis statements in Chapter 8 (pages 79–80).

Checkpoint

Think of two thesis statements that your teacher might give you for an essay. _____

_____

_____

Sometimes you must answer a **direct question**.

This sort of question looks very simple and clear. However, it is often difficult to answer because it does not tell you what point of view to take.

Some examples of direct questions are:
- What is the value of aerobic exercise?
- Should the driving age be raised?
- What is "listening"?

In addition, direct questions may not indicate what sort of information to include in the essay. It is often a good idea to ask the teacher for more information about what you should write.

You could ask your teacher questions like:
- Should I include a lot of background information?
- Should I state a lot of facts?
- How much detail should I include?
- Should I explain the reasons for each idea?

Checkpoint

Think of two direct questions that your teacher might give you for an essay. _____

_____

_____

Sometimes the 'question' is a **title** or a **subject**.

These 'questions' are similar to direct questions because they are often very general. They may not indicate what information you must include in your essay or how much you must explain

Here are some examples of title/subject 'questions':
- The development of the Impressionist movement
- The impact of immigration on land values, 1990–2006
- Volcanic activity in Japan

You must decide what point of view you want to support. Again, it is a good idea to ask for some guidelines from the teacher.

Checkpoint

Think of two titles or subjects that your teacher might give you for an essay. _____

_____

_____

Sometimes you must **complete a task**.

This sort of question is often very general because it does not tell you how much detail you should include.

For example:
* Describe the life cycle of the frog.
* Outline the stages of buyer readiness.
* Discuss three different communication models.

Usually, the technical academic words in these questions give you some guidelines about what you must do.

"Describe" and "outline" mean that you must explain some facts. "Discuss" means that you must examine some ideas and say what you think about them; you should also explain why you think in that way.

Some of these technical academic words are explained in the box below.

Technical academic words often used in essay questions

Outline	Explain the main points
Describe	Explain each point; give some details
Explain	Give the meaning; include reasons and details
Compare and contrast	Explain how two or more things are similar and/or different
Justify	Give reasons
Examine	Explain each part; show how the different parts are related
Analyse	Explain each part; show how the different parts are related
Review	Explain different ideas about a subject
Discuss	Explain different ideas about a subject; show where they are similar and different
Illustrate	Give examples
Evaluate	Explain the advantages and disadvantages of an idea; if you are comparing, show which is best

Checkpoint

Think of two tasks that your teacher might give you for an essay. _____

_____

_____

Sometimes an essay 'question' is a **mixture of styles, with several different parts**.

It may include a direct question, followed by a task. In this case you must make sure that you answer every part of the question. If you concentrate on only one part, you will lose marks.

> For example:
> What effect has television had on child health? Explain the reasons for your answer.
> This 'question' asks you to do two things. You must answer the direct question and explain the reasons for your opinions.

The essay 'question' may include a statement followed by a direct question and/or a task. Sometimes the statement is presented as a quotation.

> For example:
> - "A lower drinking age will not benefit society." Do you agree or disagree with this statement?
> - "A lower drinking age will not benefit society." Evaluate this statement.
> - "A lower drinking age will not benefit society." (Richard Prebble) Do you agree or disagree with this statement? Justify your answer.

If you have been given the name of the author of the statement, you should find out about this person. When you write your essay, it may be a good idea to explain why s/he holds that opinion. You must also think about your opinions and the thesis statement that you will use.

Checkpoint

Think of two "mixed questions" that your teacher might give you for an essay. _____

_____

_____

_____

_____

| ACTIVITY 6.1 | **Analyse an essay question.** |

Time suggested:
5–10 minutes

Use your own paper for this activity.

1   Choose an essay question from the list below (or choose your own topic).
2   Analyse the question.
   • What does the teacher want you to do?
   • What sort of information should you include?
3   When you have finished, discuss your answers with a friend.

Essay questions

a   A varied diet is an important part of keeping healthy.
b   Globalisation has had far-reaching effects on the development of our society.
c   The bicycle is a good form of transport.
d   What is the value of aerobic exercise?
e   Should the driving age be raised?
f   What is "listening"?
g   The development of _____. (Choose a subject that you know about.)
h   The impact of _____. (Choose a subject that you know about.)
i   Volcanic activity in _____. (Choose a country.)
j   Describe the life cycle of the _____. (Choose an animal or plant.)
k   Outline the stages of _____. (Choose a subject that you know about.)
l   Discuss three different _____ models. (Choose three models about the same subject.)
m   What effect has television had on child health? Explain the reasons for your answer.
n   "A lower drinking age will not benefit society."
   Do you agree or disagree with this statement?
   or
   Evaluate this statement.
   or
   Do you agree or disagree with this statement? Justify your answer.

You should also **analyse your teacher's reasons** for setting the essay. If you do this, you will understand more clearly what you have to do. You will be able to decide what information to include and how to present it.

• **Look at the learning outcomes** (or objectives) for the part of the course that you are studying. They will give guidelines about the knowledge the teacher wants to check.

• **Examine the marking schedule.** It will tell you what is required and how the teacher will award marks. It will help you decide how much research to do, or how much background information to include.

Checkpoint

Think about the last essay that you wrote (or the essay that you are writing now).

Why did your teacher set this essay? _____

What guidelines did the learning outcomes provide? _____

_____

How did the marking schedule help you to plan? _____

_____

_____

_____

Train your mind

1 Allow enough time for planning and thinking.
2 Discuss essay subjects with friends and/or family.
3 Think about essay questions while you are doing things that do not need a lot
   of concentration, e.g. housework, jogging, travelling by bus.
4 Develop good general knowledge by reading, watching television and listening
   to the radio.

Summarise the chapter

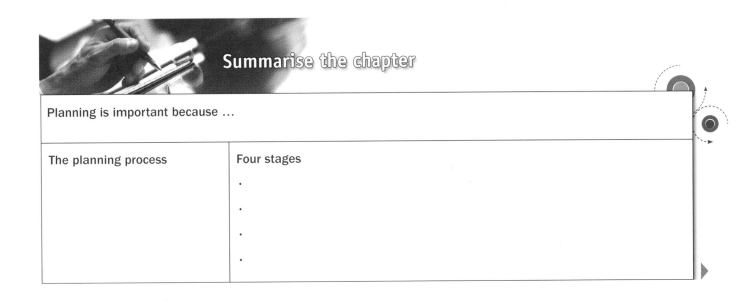

Planning is important because …		
The planning process	**Four stages**	
	•	
	•	
	•	
	•	

Cyclical model	(Use words to describe)
	(Draw a model)
Thinking is important because ...	
Analysis	Analyse questions · · · · · Analyse learning outcomes · Analyse marking schedule ·

► Check your understanding ○

Choose the correct answers.

Check whether they are correct (page 286).

If they are not correct, read the information in this chapter again.

1 Planning involves:
   a analysis, research, writing
   b analysis, finding ideas, selecting and clustering, developing an outline
   c analysis, selecting ideas, developing an outline.

2 You should always use the cyclical model of the planning process. True or false?

3 Thinking is not a separate stage in the planning process because:
   a it is not important
   b it is important only for the analysis stage
   c it is important for all the stages.

4 When you make an analysis, you must examine only the essay question. True or false?

5 If you are not sure about how to answer an essay question, you should:
   a ask your friends what they think and what they are going to write
   b ask your teacher for guidelines and for the marking schedule
   c look at the learning outcomes and ask your friends to explain them.

6 "Justify" means that you should explain the reasons for other writers' opinions and ideas. True or false?

7 A thesis statement:
   a states the subject of the essay and the writer's viewpoint
   b states why the writer thinks that the essay is useful
   c explains why the reader should agree with the writer's ideas.

8 A direct question looks easy but it is often difficult to answer. True or false?

9 If the essay question has several different parts, you should concentrate on only the first part. True or false?

10 If the essay question contains a quotation, it is a good idea to find out about the author because:
   a it may be useful to explain the reasons for his or her opinion
   b it will help to make your essay longer
   c it will make your teacher very happy.

7 Finding and organising information and ideas

When you have finished studying this chapter, you should be able to:

1 use three ways of finding information and ideas;

2 explain how to select and organise information and ideas.

There are several ways to find information and ideas.

What are the different ways?

There are at least three ways to find information and ideas. You can choose to use one way, or two, or all of them together.

> **brainstorming** thinking of as many different ideas as possible about a subject

- **Brainstorm ideas.** When you brainstorm, you think of as many different ideas as you can about a subject. This method is especially useful when you are beginning to think of ideas, or when you are writing about a simple subject.

Checkpoint

Have you used brainstorming in the past?

How did you do it? Was it useful? _____

_____

_____

> **free-writing** writing sentences about all the ideas you can think of

- **Use free-writing.** This is a bit like brainstorming. However, you write sentences about all your ideas so that the result is like a small essay.

Checkpoint

Have you ever used free-writing to think of ideas about a subject?

If so, how did you do it? Was it useful? _____

_____

_____

- **Do some research.** This involves finding information from other people about a subject. You can:
  - spend time talking to other people
  - read information that other people have written, either in printed form or on the internet
  - use audio-visual material.

researching the stage of the writing process when you find information

Checkpoint

What research have you done in the past?

What research will you need to do for the essays that you will write?

Where will you look for information and ideas? _____

_____

_____

_____

How should you brainstorm?

When you brainstorm, it is important to accept *all* ideas, even if they seem useless or silly. Sometimes a silly idea can lead to another idea that will be useful. You can decide about their usefulness later. Every idea should be written down (recorded).

It is a good idea to set a limit on the amount of brainstorming that you will do.

You can choose a target, like 20 or 25 different ideas, or a time limit, like 10 or 15 minutes.

It is important to choose a realistic limit.

If you aim for three ideas, you will not have enough; if you aim for 100 you will have too many. In the same way, five minutes may be too short and half an hour may be too long.

Of course, the limits or target that you set will depend on the subject and on the amount of time available.

You can brainstorm by yourself or with other people. A group can usually think of more ideas than a single person. If there are more than three or four people, it may be difficult to record all the ideas. If you take turns being the 'secretary', everyone has an opportunity to think of ideas. Choose a secretary who will write down everyone's ideas without deciding whether or not they are useful.

Checkpoint

Think about any brainstorming that you have done.

What did you do? How could you have improved? _____

_____

_____

_____

| **Rules for brainstorming** | • Accept and record all ideas. |
| | • Set a realistic time limit or target. |

ACTIVITY 7.1

Time suggested:
As long as you need

Brainstorm ideas.

Use your own paper for this activity.
1 Brainstorm ideas about the essay question that you analysed in Activity 6.1.
2 Work alone or with a friend (or several).
3 Set a time limit or a target.
4 Remember to accept and record all ideas.

How do you free-write?

When you free-write, you write all your thoughts as they come into your mind. Again, you should accept *every* idea. Even if an idea seems off track when you think of it, you may decide later that it is useful.

Write sentences as much as possible, so that the result looks like a small essay. When you have finished, the information will probably be disorganised; some of it may not be useful. However, this does not matter because you will have a first draft that you can work on.

Do not worry about grammar and spelling. The important thing at this stage is to record as many ideas as possible. If you keep stopping to make corrections, you will interrupt the flow of ideas. If you are using a computer, you may be distracted by seeing your typing mistakes on the screen. In this case, try turning off the computer monitor and typing with a blank screen.

It is a good idea to set a limit for free-writing, just as for brainstorming. You could set a time limit or a target, like one page or 300 words. Remember that the aim is to give you a basis for developing your essay; you do not have to write everything you know about the subject.

It is probably a good idea to free-write alone. If you are working with others, it may be difficult to record all the ideas in sentences.

Checkpoint

Think about any free-writing that you have done.

What did you do? How could you have improved? _____

_____

_____

_____

ACTIVITY 7.2   **Use free-writing to think of ideas.**

Use your own paper for this activity.

1 Do some free-writing about the essay question that you analysed in Activity 6.1.

2 Write sentences about your ideas.

3 Do not worry about grammar and spelling.

4 Try turning off the computer monitor as you write.

Time suggested:
As long as you need

What research should you do?

The research that you do depends on the essay question, and what you already know.

If the question is complicated or about a specialist subject, you will probably need to find some information.

For example, suppose you were writing an essay about the development of trade with the European Union. You would probably need to do some research because this is a specialist subject.

However, if the subject of the essay is a simple one, you may already know most of the information that you need.

If your essay was about the importance of being able to drive, you would not need to do much research. However, talking to other people might give you some extra, interesting ideas.

Even if you think that you know a lot about a subject, you should spend some time thinking and gathering ideas.

Sometimes the essay question or the marking schedule states that you must do some research. In this case, you should make sure that you allow enough time to show how well you can do this.

Checkpoint

Think about the last essay that you wrote.

How much research did you do? Was it enough?_____

_____

_____

Discussion is probably the simplest research method, although it may not be as complete or reliable as reading. However, it can help you to think more carefully about the subject or question. If you spend time talking about the question with your classmates, you will *all* develop your ideas. If you use this method, you must make sure that you write the essay on your own.

Checkpoint

Who could help you to talk about your essays?

Would they be helpful for all your essays, or would you need to talk to different people about

different subjects?_____

_____

_____

Most of your teachers will expect you to read about a subject.

You can do this by finding printed material like books, or by searching the internet. You must make sure that the information that you find is correct, and suitable for your essay.

It is easier to do this if you have already analysed the essay question.

You should keep checking that the information helps to answer the essay question. It is a very good idea to make notes about the information that you find and record where you found it.

Checkpoint

Where could you find written information for your essays? _____

_____

_____

_____

Sometimes your teachers will ask you to use audio or audio-visual material. Audio material is information that you listen to, for example radio programmes or sound tapes. Audio-visual material involves listening and seeing, like films, videos and television programmes. While you listen and/or watch, you can use the same sort of guidelines as for reading. If you are using a radio or television programme, it is a good idea to record it. Then you can make notes later and check whether they are correct. It is often expensive to buy recorded programmes from the radio or television stations.

You can find more detailed information about researching in Chapter 11 (see pages 108–121).

Checkpoint

What sorts of audio or audio-visual material would be useful for your essay research? _____

_____

ACTIVITY 7.3

Time suggested:
As long as you need

Research information.

Use your own paper for this activity.

1 Do some research about the ideas that you brainstormed in Activity 7.1 or wrote about in Activity 7.2.

2 Choose the method(s) that you will use:
   • discussion
   • reading
   • listening to audio or watching audio-visual material.

3 Find at least two pieces of relevant information or two ideas. Make sure that they are correct and reliable.

4 Discuss your answers with a friend.

You should take care when selecting and clustering.

Why is it important to take care?

Both selecting and clustering will affect the quality of your essay. When you select information and ideas, you are choosing the content of your essay. When you cluster the information, you decide which information belongs together and organise it into groups. If you do these things well, you will write a better essay. In addition, you will get better marks.

selecting choosing

clustering deciding which information belongs together and organising it into groups

How should you select?

Choose only information and ideas that are relevant. Examine everything that you have found during the research stage.

- Is it about the subject of your essay?
- Does it help to answer the question?
- Will it help to show the reader what s/he wants to know?

If you include irrelevant content in your essay, the quality of your writing will be poor and your reader will find it difficult to understand.

If you have a lot of information, choose what is most important.

> **Think about what your target reader needs to know. Remember that you may need to include information that shows your knowledge, even if the reader already knows it.**
>
> For example, if you are writing an assignment, your teacher wants to find out how much *you* understand.

> **Finally, choose any information or ideas that the target reader will find interesting or unusual or surprising.**
>
> This is especially important if you are writing an assignment. You will get better marks if you show that you have thought deeply about the subject.

How should you cluster?

You can cluster the information at the same time as you select it, although you do not have to.

Think about how the different ideas and pieces of information fit together.

- Organise them into groups (clusters).
- Add extra ideas to the clusters as you think of them.
- As you cluster the information, you will probably begin to form an opinion about the subject. This is especially useful if the essay question does not include a thesis statement.

Once you have clustered the information, you must organise each cluster.

- Consider what each cluster is about.
- Identify its main point and the supporting details.
- It is a good idea to make notes at this stage. You can use a mind map or linear notes or a table. Whichever note-making style you use, your clustered notes will form the basis of the outline of your essay. See Chapter 16 for information about making notes (pages 166–178).

ACTIVITY 7.4

Time suggested:
5–10 minutes

Select and cluster information.

Use your own paper for this activity.

1 Select and cluster the information and ideas that you recorded in Activities 7.1–7.3.
2 Discuss your answers with a friend.

Train your mind

1 Think carefully about the reasons for your ideas and opinions.
2 Keep watching and listening for new ideas (about any subject).
3 Listen especially carefully to people with ideas that are different from yours.
4 Ask other people to explain the reasons for their opinions.
5 Think about how different ideas link together.

Summarise the chapter

Finding ideas	Brainstorming
	•
	•
	•
	Free-writing
	•
	•
	•
	•
	Researching
	•
	•
	•
	•
Selecting	•
	•
	•

Clustering	 • • •

► Check your understanding

Choose the correct answers.

Check whether they are correct (page 286).

If they are not correct, read the information in this chapter again.

1 When you are finding ideas, you should:
   a use any method that is useful
   b use only two methods
   c use only one method.

2 You must always find books when you research. True or false?

3 It is often a good idea to do some research, even if you already know a lot about the essay subject. True or false?

4 When you are brainstorming ideas, you should:
   a check that your ideas are suitable for the essay
   b always work alone
   c write down as many ideas as possible.

5 When you free-write, you should write down all your ideas, even if they do not seem useful. True or false?

6 When you free-write, you should make sure that all the grammar and spelling is correct. True or false?

7 It is not necessary to check whether your teacher expects you to do some research. True or false?

8 Discussion:
   a is a useful way to find ideas, especially for simple essay subjects
   b is not really a suitable way to find information and ideas
   c should always happen at the same time as reading.

9 When you cluster, you should:
   a choose the information you will use in your essay and make notes about it
   b think about the information that you have chosen and organise it into groups
   c think about the information that you have chosen and discuss it with a group of friends.

10 When you cluster, you can add your own ideas to the information that you have collected. True or false?

8 Developing an outline for a simple expository essay

When you have finished studying this chapter, you should be able to:

1 explain the TRT formula;

2 use it to plan and write a simple expository essay.

The TRT formula is useful to plan and write a simple expository essay.

What is a simple expository essay?

A simple expository essay explains information and/or ideas about one subject. It may present information and give details about it. If it presents ideas and opinions, it explains the reasons for them.

Why is the TRT formula useful?

TRT formula a formula for planning an expository essay; includes thesis statement, response questions and topic sentences; helps the writer to keep on track

The TRT formula helps the writer keep to the topic. If you do this when you plan and write your essays, you will get better marks. It is most useful for expository essays, although it can be used for any piece of writing.

What is the TRT formula?

TRT is a mnemonic that you can use to plan an effective expository essay. The letters TRT will help you remember how to organise the essay structure, and remind you what you will achieve as a result.

Using

Thesis statement, Response question, Topic sentences

will help you to keep on

The Right Track.

> **thesis statement** a sentence that tells the reader what the essay is about and identifies the writer's point of view

The **thesis statement** is a sentence that tells the reader what the essay is about.

It is usually placed at the end of the introduction. Most tertiary-level essays require more than just facts; your teachers are interested in your opinions and the reasons why you think the way you do. Therefore a good thesis statement must have two parts: the subject of the essay and your opinion (point of view).

For example, suppose that you were writing about the value of writing academic essays. A thesis statement for this essay might be: "There are several reasons why it is important to learn to write effective academic essays."

Checkpoint

Look at the example of a thesis statement (above).

Identify the two parts: underline the subject and circle the opinion (or use different coloured highlighters).

ACTIVITY 8.1

Time suggested: 10–15 minutes

Develop some thesis statements.

1   Think of thesis statements for five different subjects. (Use the subjects in the list below, or think of your own.) Remember to include the subject and a point of view.

2   When you have finished, discuss your answers with a friend.

> **Subjects**
> a   My home town
> b   Conservation
> c   The importance of a healthy diet
> d   Culture
> e   Working in groups
>
> _____
>
> _____
>
> _____
>
> _____
>
> _____

The **response question** is what the reader might ask after reading the thesis statement.

> **response questions** what the reader might ask after reading the thesis statement

Response questions are not usually included in the essay. However, identifying them helps the writer make sure that the thesis statement is explained clearly and completely. It is a very good idea to write down the response question(s). If you do not do this, it is easy to go off track. You must make sure that the response questions are relevant to the thesis statement.

For instance, in the example about academic writing, your response question could not be: "How many words should you write in an academic essay?" That question is not relevant because it is not about the thesis statement.

You must make sure that the response questions cover all parts of the thesis statement. The number of questions you write will depend on the length of the essay. If your essay will be 2–3,000 words long, you might think of six or seven questions. However, for short essays, you will need only one or two.

In the essay about academic writing, there could be two response questions:
- What are the reasons for writing academic essays?
- Why are these reasons important?

Both of these questions are relevant and you could use them to help plan the essay.

Checkpoint

Think about the last essay that you wrote (or one that you are going to write).

What was the thesis statement? _____

_____

What was the response question (or questions)? _____

_____

_____

ACTIVITY 8.2

Develop some response questions.

1 Choose three of the thesis statements that you wrote in Activity 8.1.
2 Write two response questions for each thesis statement. Make sure that they are relevant.
3 When you have finished, discuss them with a friend.

Time suggested:
10–15 minutes

a • _____

   • _____

b • _____

   • _____

c • _____

   • _____

> topic sentence a direct answer to the response question(s); explains part or all of the thesis statement; summarises a paragraph

Topic sentences are answers to the response questions.

You should make sure that the topic sentences answer the questions in a direct way. If you do this, the essay is more likely to stay on track. Together, the topic sentences provide a complete answer to the response questions. Each topic sentence may answer only one response question and so explain part of the thesis statement.

The academic writing essay in our example could have at least five topic sentences:

- Essay writing helps students to extend their understanding of a topic.
- Many university essay topics encourage students to develop their thinking skills.
- Essay writing helps students develop good organisational skills.
- The teacher's feedback gives students information about their progress.
- Writing an essay helps students shape their thoughts and their opinions.

The outline of the essay about academic writing would look like this:

EXAMPLE 1:

Outline of an essay about the value of writing academic essays

Thesis statement:	There are several reasons why it is important to learn to write effective academic essays.
Response questions:	What are the reasons for writing academic essays? Why are these reasons important?
Topic sentences:	Essay writing helps students to extend their understanding of a topic. Many university essay topics encourage students to develop their thinking skills. Essay writing helps students to develop good organisational skills. The teacher's feedback gives students information about their progress. Writing an essay helps students to shape their thoughts and their opinions.

You can use the topic sentences to develop the body of the essay. Each topic sentence should summarise a separate paragraph. If you do this, your reader will find it easy to understand your explanation and ideas. In the next example, the body of the essay would have five paragraphs – one for each topic sentence. See Chapter 18 (pages 191–200) for information about writing paragraphs.

EXAMPLE 2:

Outline of an essay about overseas travel

Thesis statement:	Overseas travel is not always beneficial.
Response questions:	Why is overseas travel not always beneficial? What are some of the disadvantages of travelling overseas?
Topic sentences:	Overseas travel is sometimes expensive. Long-distance travel is often uncomfortable and tiring. Overseas travel can be dangerous. If you do not know another language, you may not learn much about the place you are visiting. Sightseeing in foreign countries may not help you to understand other cultures.

Checkpoint

Read Example 2 carefully.

Check that the response questions are relevant.

Check that the topic sentences answer the response questions in a direct way.

ACTIVITY 8.3   **Develop some topic sentences.**

Time suggested:
10–15 minutes

1 Choose two sets of the response questions that you wrote in Activity 8.2.
2 Write four topic sentences for each set of response questions. Make sure the topic sentences answer the response questions in a direct way.
3 When you have finished, discuss them with a friend.

a • _____

   • _____

   • _____

   • _____

b • _____

   • _____

   • _____

   • _____

You can use the TRT formula to check that your outline is on track.

How can the TRT formula be used to check your outline?

It should be possible to summarise the whole expository essay by writing the thesis statement and the topic sentences.

> If the topic sentences explain the thesis statement, the outline will be on track, and so will the whole essay.

> All the chapters in this book use the TRT formula. The response questions have been included to help you develop your thinking skills.

> It is important for you to identify and write the response questions when you plan your own essays. However, you should not include them in the final copy because you want to explain, not ask questions.

ACTIVITY 8.4

Time suggested: 10–15 minutes

Use the TRT formula to check part of Chapter 9.

Do this activity before you turn the page!
1   Look at the information marked by the dashed line in Chapter 9 (pages 90–93).
2   Identify the thesis statement, response questions and topic sentences.
3   Write them in a list.
4   Check that the response questions are relevant to the thesis statement.
5   Check whether the topic sentences answer the response questions *in a direct way*.
6   When you have finished, compare your list (outline) with Example 3 on page 86.

ACTIVITY 8.5

Time suggested: 10–15 minutes

Use the TRT formula to check your own work.

Use your own paper for this activity.
1   Choose one set of the topic sentences that you wrote in Activity 8.3.
2   Write the complete outline (thesis statement, response questions, topic sentences).
3   Use the TRT formula to check that the outline is on track.
4   Discuss your outline with a friend.

Train your mind

1   When you are reading, look for the thesis statement.
2   When you are reading, think of some response questions before you read the body of the writing.
3   Practise using the TRT formula every time you plan an expository essay.
4   Practise writing essay outlines (even if you do not write the whole essay).
5   Discuss your writing with other people.

Summarise the chapter

A simple expository essay is ...	
Reasons for using TRT	· ·
TRT formula	Two meanings · ·
Thesis statement	
Response question(s)	
Topic sentences	

EXAMPLE 3:

Outline of part of Chapter 9

Thesis statement:	You can use two different structures to organise the outline of a comparative essay.
Response questions:	What are the structures? What is the whole picture approach? What is the detailed approach? Which approach is most effective?
Topic sentences:	The two structures are the whole picture approach and the detailed approach. When you use the whole picture approach you begin by examining each idea or subject separately. When you use the detailed approach, you examine the ideas or subjects together, comparing them in the same paragraph. The two structures are useful for different purposes. The whole picture approach is probably best for simple comparisons. The detailed approach is more effective in complicated comparisons, especially where more than two subjects are being compared.

► Check your understanding

Choose the correct answers.

Check whether they are correct (page 286).

If they are not correct, read the information in this chapter again.

1 A simple expository essay is:
   a writing that exposes information and ideas about a subject
   b writing that puts information and ideas into the correct position
   c writing that explains information and ideas about a subject.

2 You can use the TRT formula to help you to organise an essay. True or false?

3 TRT stands for:
   a **T**opic statement, **R**eaction, **T**hesis sentence
   b **T**hesis statement, **R**esponse question, **T**opic sentence
   c The **R**ight **T**hesis statement.

4 A thesis statement has two parts. It tells the reader about:
   a the subject of the essay and why the subject is interesting
   b the subject of the essay and the writer's point of view
   c the subject of the essay and whether the reader will enjoy reading the essay.

5 A response question is:
   a what the reader might ask when s/he has read the thesis statement
   b what the writer wants the reader to know
   c what the reader might ask after reading the essay.

6   The response questions should cover all parts of the thesis statement. True or false?

7   The response questions are usually included in the final copy of the essay. True or false?

8   The topic sentences:
    a   should answer the thesis statement in a direct way
    b   should answer the response questions in a direct way
    c   should ask the questions that the reader might want to know.

9   The topic sentences should include all the details about the essay subject. True or false?

10   Together, the topic sentences should answer all the response questions. True or false?

9 Developing an outline for a comparative essay

Learning outcomes

When you have finished studying this chapter, you should be able to:

1 use the TRT formula to develop the outline of a simple comparative essay

2 explain two different ways of organising a comparative essay.

You can adapt the TRT formula to plan a comparative essay.

What is a comparative essay?

A comparative essay examines two or more ideas or pieces of information and identifies their similarities and differences. While it is a type of expository essay, it has two purposes: it must compare as well as explain. Sometimes, the writer must decide which idea is better or more useful.

How can you use TRT for a comparative essay?

When you develop the outline, you should use the same process as for a simple expository essay. You should:

- identify or develop the thesis statement
- think of some relevant response questions
- make the topic sentences answer the response questions in a direct way.

You must also organise them logically so that the reader will find your explanation easy to understand.

What must you change?

A comparative essay examines more than one idea or subject, so the structure is a little more complicated.

The thesis statement and response questions are more complicated than for a simple expository essay. We will consider two examples: an essay about Australia, and one about university. The thesis statements and response questions for simple expository essays on these subjects might look like this:

Australia

Thesis statement:
Australia is an interesting tourist destination

Response question:
Why is Australia interesting for tourists?

University

Thesis statement:
University study provides students with a challenge

Response question:
What are the challenges that students face at university?

In a comparative essay, the thesis statement must show what you are comparing as well as your point of view. The response questions are also likely to be more complicated, and there may be more of them. For example:

Australia

Thesis statement:
Australia is a more interesting tourist destination than New Zealand.

Response questions:
What interesting things are in Australia?
What interesting things are in New Zealand?
Why is Australia more interesting for tourists than New Zealand?

University

Thesis statement:
University is different from school.

Response questions:
What is university like?
What is school like?
What are the differences?

If you are comparing more than two things in an essay, your thesis statement and response questions must show this:

Australia, New Zealand and Singapore

Thesis statement:
Australia is a more interesting tourist destination than New Zealand or Singapore.

Response questions:
What interesting things are in Australia?
What interesting things are in New Zealand?
What interesting things are in Singapore?
Why is Australia more interesting for tourists than both the other places?

University

Thesis statement:
University, polytechnic and school have important differences.

Response questions:
What is university like?
What is polytechnic like?
What is school like?
What are the differences?
Why are they important?

As a result, the structure of a comparative essay is more complicated than for simple expository writing.

ACTIVITY 9.1

Time suggested:
20–30 minutes

Begin to develop an outline for a comparative essay.

Use your own paper for this activity.

1 Write a thesis statement and response question(s) for five different comparisons.
2 You can include similarities or differences or both.
3 Make sure that every thesis statement includes both subjects and a point of view. You can use the subjects in the list below, or think of your own.
4 When you have finished, discuss your answers with a friend.

Subjects

a Festivals in two different cultures, e.g. Chinese Spring Festival and Christmas in New Zealand
b Two seasons, e.g. spring and autumn
c Two forms of transport, e.g. bicycles and cars
d Two television programmes
e Two writing genres

You can use two different structures to organise the outline of a comparative essay.

What are the structures?

The two structures are:

• the whole picture approach, and
• the detailed approach.

What is the whole picture approach?

whole picture approach
an essay structure that
examines different ideas or
subjects separately, then
compares them

When you use the whole picture approach, you begin by examining each idea or subject separately.

You compare them after you have analysed or explained both of them.

If you were comparing Australia and New Zealand, you could write about Australia first, then about New Zealand. You might plan several paragraphs about each country, for example:
• a paragraph about things to do
• a paragraph about the scenery
• a paragraph about culture.
Then you would identify the main similarities and differences, and show that Australia was the most interesting. You could use the same sort of structure to compare university and school.

Your outline for the Australia/New Zealand essay would look like this:

EXAMPLE 1:

Outline of a comparative essay using the whole picture approach

Thesis statement:	Australia is a more interesting tourist destination than New Zealand.
Response questions:	What interesting things are in Australia?
	What interesting things are in New Zealand?
	Why is Australia more interesting for tourists than New Zealand?

Topic sentences:

Several sentences about Australia:	There are a lot of interesting activities to do in Australia.
	The scenery in Australia is spectacular and very varied.
	Australia has many different cultures.
Several sentences about New Zealand:	New Zealand also offers some exciting and interesting activities.
	While there is a lot of beautiful countryside in New Zealand, there is less variety.
	New Zealand also has many different cultures.
A sentence that compares Australia and New Zealand:	While Australia and New Zealand are both interesting places, Australia has a greater variety of scenery.

Checkpoint

If you used the whole picture approach for the university/school example, what would the essay outline look like? _____

_____

_____

ACTIVITY 9.2

Time suggested:
20–30 minutes

Develop topic sentences for the whole picture approach.

Use your own paper for this activity.

1   Choose two sets of thesis statement/response questions that you wrote in Activity 9.1.

2   Use the whole picture approach and write six topic sentences for each set.

3   Make sure that the topic sentences answer the response questions in a direct way.

4   When you have finished, discuss them with a friend.

What is the detailed approach?

> **detailed approach** an essay structure that uses each paragraph to examine a single point about two or more ideas or subjects

When you use the detailed approach, you examine the ideas or subjects together, comparing them in the same paragraph. Each topic sentence is about a single point (detail). In the Australia/New Zealand example, your topic sentences would be about:

- things to do in Australia and New Zealand
- the scenery in Australia and New Zealand
- the cultures in Australia and New Zealand.

In this case, your essay outline would look like this:

EXAMPLE 2:

Outline of a comparative essay using the detailed approach

Thesis statement:	Australia is a more interesting tourist destination than New Zealand.
Response questions:	What interesting things are in Australia? What interesting things are in New Zealand? Why is Australia more interesting for tourists than New Zealand?
Topic sentences:	There are lots of activities to do in both Australia and New Zealand. While both countries have beautiful scenery, there is more variety in Australia. Both countries have many different cultures.

It would be easy to include examples about a third country in each paragraph.

Checkpoint

If you used the detailed approach for the university/polytechnic/school example, what would the essay structure look like? _____

_____

_____

ACTIVITY 9.3   **Develop topic sentences for the detailed approach.**

Time suggested:
20–30 minutes

Use your own paper for this activity

1   Choose two sets of thesis statement/response questions that you wrote in Activity 9.1. You can use the ones you used for Activity 9.2, or choose different ones.

2   Write three topic sentences for each set. Make sure that the topic sentences answer the response questions in a direct way.

3   When you have finished, discuss them with a friend.

Which approach is most effective?

The two structures are useful for different purposes. You should choose whichever approach best suits the essay that you are writing and the reader that you are writing for.

The whole picture approach is probably best for simple comparisons. Do not use it for more than two subjects, or when there is a lot of information about each subject. This is because the reader must remember all the information in order to understand the conclusion.

The detailed approach is more effective in complicated comparisons, especially where more than two subjects are being compared. This is because the reader can understand the similarities and differences, from the beginning.

Checkpoint

Look at the part of this chapter that has been marked with a dashed line (pages 90–93).

It compares two different ways of organising a comparative essay.

Does it use a whole picture or a detailed approach?

ACTIVITY 9.4   **Write the outline of a comparative essay.**

Time suggested:
10–15 minutes

Use your own paper for this activity.

1   Choose one set of topic sentences that you wrote in Activity 9.3 or 9.4.

2   Write the complete outline (thesis statement, response questions, topic sentences) for the essay.

3   Use the TRT formula to check that the outline is on track.

4   When you have finished, discuss your answers with a friend.

Train your mind

1 Discuss ideas with friends and family.
2 Practise thinking of thesis statements.
3 When you are reading, think of some response questions before you read the body of the writing.
4 Think about how things are similar and different, e.g. objects, ideas, people.
5 Practise writing comparative essay outlines (even if you do not write the whole essay).

Summarise the chapter

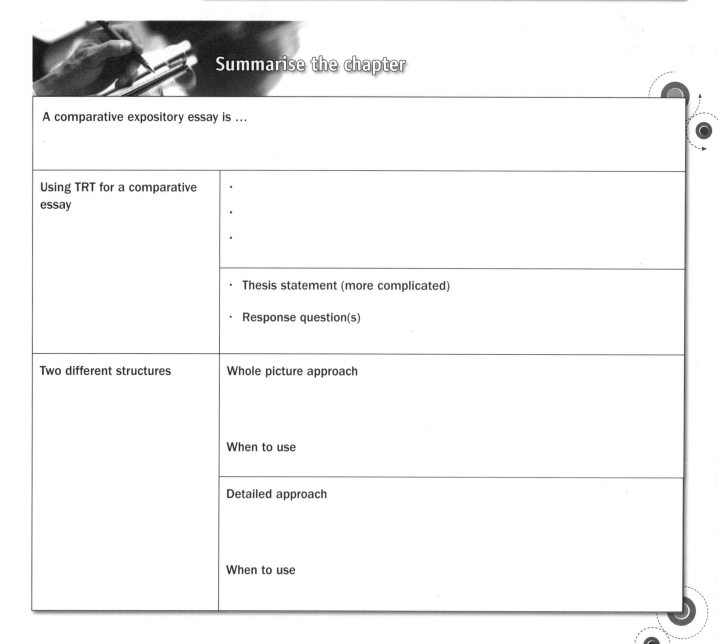

A comparative expository essay is …	
Using TRT for a comparative essay	· · ·
	· Thesis statement (more complicated) · Response question(s)
Two different structures	**Whole picture approach** **When to use**
	Detailed approach **When to use**

► Check your understanding

Choose the correct answers.
Check whether they are correct (page 286).
If they are not correct, read the information in this chapter again.

1   A comparative essay is:
   a   another name for a simple expository essay
   b   a type of expository essay
   c   a type of argumentative essay.

2   A comparative essay is more complicated than a simple expository essay because it has three purposes. True or false?

3   In a comparative essay, the thesis statement must include:
   a   what you are comparing and your point of view
   b   what you are comparing
   c   your opinions and one of the things you are examining.

4   A comparative essay often uses more response questions than a simple expository essay. True or false?

5   When you use the whole picture approach, you must:
   a   always write about Australia first
   b   examine each idea or subject separately, then identify the similarities and differences
   c   write topic sentences that compare both ideas or subjects together.

6   The detailed approach has more details than the whole picture approach. True or false?

7   In the detailed approach, each topic sentence must be about:
   a   a separate idea or subject, with a lot of examples
   b   the scenery or the culture of one place
   c   a single detail about two different ideas or subjects.

8   The whole picture approach and the detailed approach are suitable for different purposes. True or false?

9   The detailed approach is most suitable for:
   a   comparing more than two ideas or subjects
   b   very simple comparisons
   c   any sort of comparison.

10   The whole picture approach is most suitable for complicated comparisons. True or false?

10 Developing an outline for an argumentative essay

Learning outcomes

When you have finished studying this chapter, you should be able to:

1. explain how to choose which point of view to support;

2. explain the classical structure;

3. develop an outline for an argumentative essay.

Argumentative writing has a special structure.

Why does it have a special structure?

Argumentative writing is about issues.

issue a subject that people have different opinions about

An issue is a subject that people have different opinions about.

For example, there is an issue in Western society about whether children should be allowed to eat junk food*. Some people say that it is bad for their health; others believe that children should be allowed to choose what they eat.

An argumentative essay presents a point of view in a persuasive way. That is, it encourages the reader to accept and agree with the writer's ideas.

It would be difficult to write an argumentative essay about the ingredients in junk food. Most of the information would be facts, so an expository essay would be more suitable. However, an argumentative essay about junk food could try to persuade the reader that:
- junk food is bad for health

or
- children should not eat it.

---

*Junk food is food and drink that is not healthy. It often contains a lot of sugar, fat or salt. Many take-away foods are in this category.

You can find more information about argumentative writing in Chapter 3 (pages 29–37).

(pages 29–37)

↓*Checkpoint*

Think of another issue about junk food (or choose an issue about another subject). _____

_____

What should you include?

Like an expository essay, an argumentative essay must contain a clear introduction, body and conclusion.

- The paragraphs in the body have topic sentences which are placed consistently and in a logical order.
- Each paragraph must be about one part of the discussion and must answer a response question in a direct way.

An argumentative essay usually includes some explanation, so you can use the TRT formula to help you to develop an outline. See Chapter 8 for information about the TRT formula (pages 79–87).

The thesis statement may include the words "should" or "must" because you want to be persuasive.

In the junk food example, the thesis statements for the argumentative essays could be:
- You should not eat junk food.
- Children should not be allowed to eat junk food.

ACTIVITY 10.1

Time suggested: 5–10 minutes

Develop thesis statements for an argumentative essay.

1   Think about the issue that you identified in the last checkpoint.
2   Develop two thesis statements about the issue.
3   Check that each one includes the subject and a strong viewpoint.
4   When you have finished, discuss with a friend.

_____

_____

_____

_____

It is important to develop some response questions, because they will help you to justify your ideas and keep your writing on track.

> **The response questions for an argumentative essay often begin with "why".**
>
> > For instance, some of the response questions for the junk food example could be:
> > - Why should you avoid junk food?
> > - Why should children be forbidden to eat junk food?

ACTIVITY 10.2

Time suggested: 5–10 minutes

Develop some response questions.

Use your own paper for this activity.
1. Draw a line down the centre of a piece of paper.
2. At the top of each column, write one of the thesis statements that you developed in Activity 10.1.
3. Write response questions below each thesis statement.
4. Discuss your answers with a friend.

Sometimes you must decide which point of view to support.

When do you have to decide?

Sometimes, teachers offer a choice of essay questions.

> **They might give you two opposing viewpoints about the same issue.**
>
> > In the junk food example, the opposing thesis statements could be:
> > - Junk food should not be sold in schools
> >
> > and
> > - Schools should be allowed to sell whatever sort of food they choose.

checkpoint

Look at the thesis statements that you listed in Activity 10.1. Check that they have opposing meanings. If they do not, change one so that they are opposite.

How can you decide which point of view to support?

You should choose as quickly as possible. Many people spend a lot of time choosing the 'right' thesis statement. Once they have decided, they may have problems thinking about enough ideas to answer the response questions. Then they change their minds and choose the opposite viewpoint, or even a different subject. As a result, they do not spend enough time writing, so their essay is not effective.

Checkpoint

How do you choose an essay subject? Do you find it easy or difficult?

You need to develop strategies to help you avoid these problems. Your teacher probably doesn't mind which thesis statement you choose. S/he is more interested in how you write and how you present and support your ideas. If you can find a way to make a quick decision, you can spend more time on writing.

It is a good idea to begin by spending some time thinking. You can do this on your own, maybe writing down some ideas. You might also read about the subject, especially if it is complicated or new for you.

It is also useful to discuss the issue with other people.

- Ask each other for the reasons behind your opinions.
- Listen carefully to other people's ideas, even if you disagree strongly.

Perhaps you should listen carefully *especially* if you disagree strongly. Remember that you want to learn as much as possible about the subject.

While you are thinking and discussing, you can also begin to plan. You can make a table to organise your ideas and develop possible outlines for both sides of the argument. Here is an example:

 EXAMPLE 1:

Possible outline for junk food essay

Thesis statement:

| Junk food should not be sold in schools. | Schools should be allowed to sell whatever sort of food they choose. |

Response questions:

| Why should junk food be banned from schools? What harm does junk food do? | Why should schools be allowed this choice? What are the advantages of allowing choice? |

Against junk food:	**In favour of giving children a choice:**
• Eating junk food causes children to become overweight.	• Junk food is delicious and children like eating it.
• A lot of junk food contains additives that affect children's ability to concentrate and learn.	• There is no harm in eating junk food occasionally.
• Schools have a responsibility to look after the welfare of their students while they are at school.	• Food sales are an important source of income for many schools.
	• Banning junk food from school shops will not stop children from buying it.
• Many children do not have the knowledge or experience to make sensible eating choices.	• Learning to make responsible choices is an important part of a child's education.

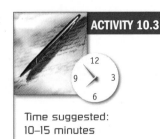

ACTIVITY 10.3

Time suggested:
10–15 minutes

Think of ideas about an issue.

Use your own paper for this activity.

1   Think of ideas to support the thesis statements and response questions that you developed in Activities 10.1 and 10.2.

2   Add your ideas to the table that you began to develop.

3   When you have finished, discuss your answers with other people.

Once you have organised the ideas, you can consider which 'side' to choose. Sometimes you can choose the point of view with the most ideas. However, you should also think about quality. It may be better to choose a viewpoint with a smaller number of strong ideas. It is not always good to choose the point of view that you agree with. Sometimes your reason for writing is to show how well you can write an essay.

You can use the classical structure to organise an argumentative essay.

What is the classical structure?

classical structure
organisation of an
argumentative essay
that uses confirmation,
concession and refutation

The classical structure uses three different sorts of paragraph to organise the body of the essay. They are:

• confirmation

• concession

• refutation.

What is confirmation?

confirmation support for the
thesis statement

Confirmation paragraphs support the thesis statement, just as for an expository essay.

> They must also answer the response question(s) in a direct way.

> > For example, suppose that you were arguing that junk food should not be sold in schools. Your confirmation paragraphs might discuss the health problems that junk food causes, and the effects it has on children.

> The content (information) is often similar to the information in an expository essay. However, the words that you use should be more persuasive.

See Chapter 17, pages 186–188, for information about writing persuasively.

ACTIVITY 10.4   **Develop some confirmation topic sentences.**

Time suggested:
10 minutes

Use your own paper for this activity.

1 Consider the table that you developed in Activity 10.3.

2 Decide which thesis statement to write about.

3 Develop three or four topic sentences that could be used for confirmation paragraphs. Make sure that they answer the response question(s) in a direct way.

4 When you have finished, discuss your answers with a friend.

What is concession?

Concession paragraphs discuss the opposite point of view. This means that you should recognise and explain (concede) that other people have different opinions. At tertiary level, your teachers want you to show that you can think critically. You can do this by examining different opinions that people have about an issue.

> **concession** recognition of someone else's point of view

You should choose the most important and strongest idea that disagrees with your point of view.

Explain the main points of this opinion and give some details or examples.

> In the junk food essay, your concession paragraph might explain that junk food tastes good and many people like it. You might also suggest that occasionally eating junk food does not cause any harm.

You can use transition signals to emphasise the concession and show that you are explaining an opposing point of view.

> Use phrases like:
> - on the other hand
> - some people might argue that …
> - it is true that …

You can find more detailed information about transition signals in Chapter 20 (pages 213–223).

ACTIVITY 10.5   **Develop a concession topic sentence.**

Time suggested:
10–15 minutes

Use your own paper for this activity.

1 Look at the table that you developed in Activity 10.3.

2 Choose the strongest idea that disagrees with the thesis statement that you chose in Activity 10.4.

3 Develop a topic sentence that could be used for a concession paragraph. Make sure that it disagrees with the confirmation.

4 When you have finished, discuss your answers with a friend.

If you are not careful, your concession paragraph may persuade the reader to ignore your confirmation paragraphs.

If it contradicts your confirmation paragraphs very effectively, it may overcome them.

In the example about junk food, the concession might persuade the reader that it is alright to eat junk food.

Therefore, you must include a refutation paragraph.

What is refutation?

refutation (rebuttal)
statements that overcome an opposite viewpoint

Refutation (sometimes called rebuttal) explains why the ideas in the concession are not as good as the opinions in your confirmation. You refute (or rebut) the concession. If you refute the strongest opposing idea convincingly, you will overcome the opposition.

An effective refutation includes an explanation and extra details or examples.

It is a bit like an extra confirmation, except that it focuses on the concession.

In the junk food example, your refutation might explain that many children eat a lot of junk food, not a little. You might also say that schools must teach children about healthy eating and so they should not sell junk food.

Again, you can use transition signals to guide the reader.

For instance you could use words and phrases like:
· however
· this view is misguided because ...
· this idea does not take into account that ....

ACTIVITY 10.6

Time suggested:
10–15 minutes

Develop a refutation.

Use your own paper for this activity.
1 Consider the concession you developed in Activity 10.5.
2 Think of why the reader should not believe or accept this idea.
3 Write a topic sentence that could be used for a refutation. Make sure that it agrees with the confirmation paragraphs that you developed in Activity 10.4.
4 When you have finished, discuss your answers with a friend.

You can organise the classical structure in different ways.

How can you organise the classical structure?

In a short essay, you can use a **simple classical structure**. You can present the confirmation paragraphs first, followed by the concession and the refutation. You might have several confirmation paragraphs and one combined concession-refutation paragraph. If you used a simple classical structure for the junk food example, the topic sentences in your outline would look like this:

Topic sentences

Several confirmation sentences: Eating junk food causes children to become overweight.
A lot of junk food contains additives that affect children's ability to concentrate and learn.
Schools have a responsibility to look after the welfare of their students.
Many children do not have the knowledge or experience to make sensible eating choices.

A concession sentence: Some people argue that there is no harm in eating junk food occasionally.

A refutation sentence: However, many children eat a lot of junk food, not a little.

ACTIVITY 10.7

Time suggested: 15–20 minutes

Use the classical structure to develop an outline for a short argumentative essay.

Use your own paper for this activity.
1   Consider your answers for Activities 10.1–10.6.
2   Use them to write a new outline for an argumentative essay.
3   Use the TRT formula to check that the confirmation and refutation are on track.
4   Make sure that the concession does not agree with the thesis statement.
5   When you have finished, discuss your answers with a friend.

In a long essay, you might want to **include several concessions**. In this case, you should place each refutation after the concession that it overcomes. The concession and refutation topic sentences in your outline might look like this.

A concession sentence: Some people argue that there is no harm in eating junk food occasionally.

A refutation sentence: Many children eat a lot of junk food, not a little.

A concession sentence: Banning junk food from school shops will not stop children from buying it.

A refutation sentence: Schools have a responsibility to look after the welfare of their students while they are at school.

This sort of organisation can be very effective. However, it is more difficult than a simple classical structure. If you want to try this method, you can use the next activity to practise. If you prefer to use the simple structure, move to the summarising activity!

ACTIVITY 10.8

Time suggested:
20–30 minutes

Use the classical structure to develop an outline for a long essay.

Use your own paper for this activity.

1   Consider the outline that you developed in Activity 10.7.
2   Choose some extra concession points from the table that you developed in Activity 10.3.
3   Think of a refutation for each concession. (You may need to use some of the confirmation points.)
4   Write a new outline, showing the extra topic sentences for the concessions and refutations.
5   Use the TRT formula to check that the confirmation and refutations are on track.
6   Make sure that the concessions do not agree with the thesis statement.
7   When you have finished, discuss your answers with a friend.

Train your mind

1   Discuss your ideas with other people (but write your essay alone).
2   Observe how other people organise persuasive talking.
3   When you read, identify the structure that the writer uses.
4   When you are talking or reading, think about issues and different viewpoints.
5   Practise writing essay outlines (even if you do not write the essays).

Summarise the chapter

Argumentative writing is …	
An issue is …	
Use the TRT formula	• Thesis statement • Response question(s) • Topic sentences
Choose a point of view to support	• • • • •
The classical structure	• Confirmation • Concession • Refutation
Simple classical structure (short essay)	
Extra concessions (long essay)	

► Check your understanding ○

Choose the correct answers.
Check whether they are correct (page 286).
If they are not correct, read the information in this chapter again.

1 Argumentative writing aims to persuade the reader to have an argument with the writer. True or false?

2 When we are talking about argumentative writing, an 'issue' is:
   a part of a newspaper
   b a subject that everyone agrees about
   c a subject that people often disagree about.

3 When you choose an essay question, you should:
   a choose the first one on the list
   b choose the one that you have the best ideas about
   c choose the one that you agree with.

4 You can use the TRT formula to help you organise the confirmation paragraphs. True or false?

5 A confirmation sentence contains information and ideas that disagree with the thesis statement. True or false?

6 A concession sentence contains information and ideas that:
   a agree with the thesis statement
   b disagree with the thesis statement
   c overcome opposing ideas.

7 It does not matter which point of view you choose for a concession paragraph. True or false?

8 A refutation sentence should never follow a concession. True or false?

9 A refutation:
   a overcomes the concession
   b overcomes the confirmation
   c overcomes the thesis statement.

10 In a long essay, you might want to use more than one concession/refutation. True or false?

SECTION

5

Researching

This section discusses how to find and evaluate information and ideas from other people. It also gives suggestions about reading effectively and making notes.

11 Research methods

When you have finished studying this chapter, you should be able to:

1 explain the reasons for researching information;

2 explain how to decide what you need to find out;

3 explain three ways to research information.

Research is an important part of writing academic essays.

What is research?

Research involves finding information and ideas from other people. You can do this in three ways. You can use:

- oral communication (talking and listening)
- audio and/or audio-visual material
- written material.

Sometimes the research process overlaps with planning, especially when you find new ideas to include in your essays.

Checkpoint

Think of the last essay that you wrote (or the one that you are writing now).

What sort of research did you need to do? _____

_____

_____

Why do you need to research?

Learning and thinking are probably the most important reasons for researching information. They often happen at the same time. Learning is more than just hearing or reading. It involves accepting information and ideas, and understanding and remembering them. As you discuss or watch or read, you will often find information and ideas that are new for you. If you think carefully about them, you will learn more, and you will develop new ideas of your own. As a result, you will find the subject interesting, and you will enjoy finding more information. We can use cyclical and spiral models to explain this process. A cyclical model might look like this:

learning accepting information and ideas, and understanding and remembering them

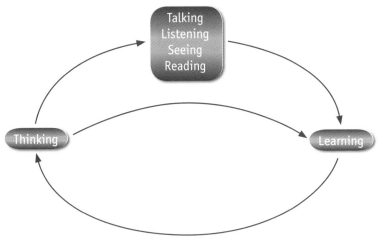

Figure 11.1 Cyclical model of the research process

We can use a spiral model to show how your skills might keep improving while you are finding information. It would look like this:

spiral model a description of a process that improves a situation

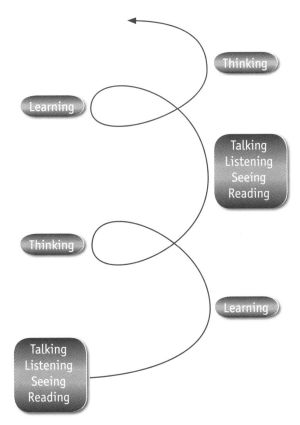

Figure 11.2 Spiral model of the research process

ACTIVITY 11.1

Time suggested:
5–10 minutes

Think about your learning and thinking.

1 Think about the last time that you discovered new information.
2 Did your learning and thinking encourage you to find out more?
3 Write two or three sentences, or draw a diagram in the space below.
4 Explain your description or diagram to a friend.

Another reason for research is to support your statements and ideas.

If you explain where you found information, your reader can check it.

> Suppose that you were writing an essay about different learning styles. You could ask your friends to tell you about how they like to learn. However, your reader might find it difficult to check the information.

If you show that other people have the same ideas as you, then your argument will be stronger.

> However, your reader might not know your friends and would not have any reason to believe them.

It is therefore a good idea to use information and ideas from experts or specialists.

> If you found information from someone who is knowledgeable about learning, your reader would have more reason to accept the information. In addition, s/he would find it easier to check.

If you do this, your reader will be more likely to accept what you say.

Checkpoint

Think of the last essay that you wrote (or the one that you are writing now).

What sort of information did you use to support your statements and ideas? _____

_____

_____

You might also do some research to show that you have good research skills. At tertiary level, you must often learn about theory and principles that other people have developed. In addition, you must think deeply about others' ideas. Your teachers expect you to find a lot of this information for yourself and they want you to show how well you can do this.

Begin by deciding what you need to find out.

Why should you do this?

You will save time if you know what you want to find out, before you start researching. This is because:

- you will be able to think about where to find information
- you will not waste time looking at information that is not useful or relevant
- you will keep on track more easily.

How do you decide what you need to find out?

A list of questions makes your research task much easier.

Your list will be more useful if you have already done some planning.

For example, suppose that your essay question was:

"Students should consider their preferred learning styles when organising their study." Do you agree or disagree with this statement? Justify your answer.

Your analysis of the question will tell you what sort of information to look for.

You know that "justify" means "give reasons". Therefore, you know that you must look for information about why learning styles are important (or not important).

The response questions in your outline are also useful. These questions are often quite simple. However, you must keep them in mind while you are researching.

The response questions for our example could be:
- What are learning styles?
- How do they affect study?
- Should students consider them or ignore them?
- Why?

Information that does not help you to answer the response questions is not useful for your essay.

Although you should keep on track with your research, you should also be prepared to be flexible.

> If you find information that does not answer one of your research or response questions, you should consider whether it is relevant. If it is not relevant, then you should not use it.

>> For instance, when you read about learning styles, you might find an explanation of different styles. This could be useful and relevant for your essay, because you could use the information for your examples. However, your response questions do not ask about the different styles.

> You should consider whether the information answers a useful response question that you did not think of before.

>> You could add an extra response question to the outline of the learning styles essay: What are the different sorts of learning style? You would also add it to your list of research questions.

> If you do this, you are more likely to show your reader that you have thought deeply about the subject.

(See Chapter 8, pages 79–87, for information about response questions.)

ACTIVITY 11.2

Time suggested:
20–30 minutes

Develop some research questions.

Use your own paper for this exercise.

1   Choose an essay question. You can use the question that you analysed in Chapter 6, or you can choose a new one.
2   Develop a list of research questions. Use your analysis of the question, and the response questions, to help you.
3   Discuss your list with a friend.

Decide what methods to use.

Which research methods should you use?

The method(s) that you choose will depend on the essay subject.

> If the essay is about an issue that is important at the moment, you could find out what other people think.

>> You could:
>> • find relevant information in newspapers, or on television or the radio
>> • attend a public meeting where there are guest speakers who are knowledgeable about the subject.

If the subject is related to your study, it may be easier and better to find written information from specialist books or websites.

Checkpoint

Think of an issue that is important at the moment.

What methods could you use to find information about this issue? _____

_____

_____

In addition, you should consider your level of study. Generally, interviews and discussion are more suitable for simple essays, or when you do not need specialist information. However, they are sometimes – but not always – less reliable than written information. Your teachers will often expect you to read for information.

Checkpoint

Think about the essays that you write.

What research methods are suitable for your level of study? _____

_____

_____

The method that you choose might also depend on how you prefer to learn. People often learn most effectively if they use their preferred learning style: seeing or reading or listening or being active. This does not mean that they cannot learn or think in other ways. Your learning style might be important if you have a strong preference. It might be worthwhile to look for some information that is presented in a way that is suitable for you. There is more information about learning styles in Chapter 1, pages 5–6.

Checkpoint

How do you prefer to learn?

How will this affect your research? _____

_____

_____

Oral communication is one way to find information.

What is oral communication?

Oral communication is any way of finding information that involves talking or listening to people. You could choose:

- a discussion
- an interview
- a lecture.

How should you use oral communication to find information?

You should talk to people who may have useful ideas.

A discussion with your friends or family is often useful when you are looking for general information and ideas.

> For the learning styles essay, you could have a dinnertime conversation about:
> - how each person likes to learn
> - why some people like school and others do not
> - why some people like listening to the radio but others prefer watching television.

Ask questions that are suitable for the people you are talking to.

> For example, a small child will not have many ideas about learning styles, but could talk about what s/he likes doing at school.

Choose a suitable time for your discussion.

> Someone who is already late for a meeting will not be happy to talk. You may need to make a time to talk later.

In an informal discussion, you should make notes after the conversation has finished. You want lots of information and ideas, so it is not a good idea to interrupt the flow.

If you talk to your classmates, you are more likely to discuss the essay subject in more detail.

You can compare the information that everyone has found.

> For example, you might each explain a different learning style; or you might discuss why different people have different preferences.

This sort of discussion can be very useful for sharing information and ideas.

You might all want to make notes while you are talking.

However, you must always write the essay on your own, unless your teacher tells you otherwise.

An interview with a specialist often is very useful.

If you do this, you should find someone who is knowledgeable and good at explaining.

For instance, you could talk to a teacher about learning styles.

It is a good idea to keep discussions short and on track. If you do this, people will be willing to spend time on a different discussion for your next essay. If the person is very busy, having a list of questions prepared will help to avoid wasting their time.

If you are listening to a speaker, you may want to tape what is said.

You do not usually need to ask permission for a public meeting. However, you should ask permission if the meeting is private.

For instance, you should ask permission to tape a university lecture or a presentation at a sports club. If you are taping a telephone conversation, it is polite to tell the other person.

Taping allows you to check your notes afterwards and make sure you have recorded all the important information.

ACTIVITY 11.3   **Use oral communication to find information.**

Use your own paper for this activity.

1   Choose an oral research method.
2   Use this method to find answers to some of the research questions that you developed in Activity 11.2.
3   Make notes about the answers.
4   Discuss your notes with a friend.

Time suggested:
As long as you need

You can use audio and audio-visual materials for research.

What are audio and audio-visual materials?

audio material information that you listen to

audio-visual material information that you listen to and watch at the same time

- Audio material is information that you listen to, for example radio programmes, listening tapes or CDs.
- Audio-visual material is information that you listen to and watch at the same time, like television programmes, videos or DVDs.

Television and radio programmes are often useful for essays about issues that are important at the time you are writing. Sometimes you can borrow educational videos or DVDs from the library.

How should you use audio or audio-visual material to find information?

You should listen or watch the material as many times as you need, to find answers to your research questions.

- Begin by watching or listening to gain general understanding. If you tape television or radio programmes, you can check details later.
- Do not waste time watching or listening to something that is not relevant. Use the fast forward button and "skim watch" or "skim listen" to see if there is any useful information. If the essay question is about a specific film or programme, you should watch all of it.
- Make notes while you watch or listen. Use the pause button so that you can list all the information that you need.

ACTIVITY 11.4

Time suggested:
As long as you need

Use audio or audio-visual material to find information.

Use your own paper for this activity.

1 Choose the sort of material to use.
2 Use it to find answers to some of the research questions that you developed in Activity 11.2.
3 Make notes about the answers.
4 Discuss your notes with a friend.

Written material is probably the most commonly used for research.

What is written material?

written material any information that contains words or pictures

hard copy written material that has been printed

Written material is any information that contains words or pictures. It can include "hard copy", that is, something that has been printed so that you can hold it.

Examples are:

- books
- newspapers
- magazines
- journals.

It can also be "soft copy", that is, the words or pictures have not been printed. You can look at soft copy, but you cannot hold it. Examples are:

- information that you see on a website or in a chat room
- an article in an electronic journal
- an essay, which has not yet been printed, that you have written on the computer.

soft copy written material that is recorded electronically and has not been printed

Why is written material used more than other types of material?

If you are studying at a university or polytechnic, reading is the traditional way of finding information. There are two main reasons for this.

Written material is an easy way for people to share ideas. This was especially true before electronic technology was developed.

The internet and e-mail are less than 30 years old. Before they were developed, printed material was the best way to spread information.

Your teachers can check written material more quickly and easily than the other types of material.

Teachers can skim-read a written text more quickly than they can search through audio-visual material. They can check a text more easily than a discussion or interview.

Where can you find written information?

You may be able to find useful information on your own or your friends' bookshelves.

For academic essays, your textbooks are the most obvious places to begin looking. Your study notes should also be useful.

For the learning styles essay, you may have some written information about study skills.

You can ask other people whether they have any suitable information.

For example, you might know someone who is interested in the subject.

Libraries are the next places to look.

Choose a library that is likely to have material at a suitable level for your essay. For tertiary study, a university or polytechnic library will often be more useful than a general public library.

However, many people are interested in learning styles, so you could probably find relevant information about this subject in your local library.

For very specialised subjects, you may need to find a specialist library.

For example, if you were writing about rare tropical diseases, you might need to look in a specialist medical library.

If you know how to use the library catalogue, it will be easier to find suitable information.

Checkpoint

Do you know how to use the catalogue in the libraries that you will use?

If not, how can you learn this skill? _____

_____

The internet has a huge amount of information.

It often has much more information than you need or can manage.

If you do a general search about learning styles on the internet, you will find more than 9 000 000 pieces of information! If you have this amount of information, it is almost impossible to decide what is most useful.

In addition, information from websites and chat rooms is often unreliable. This is because anyone can place material on the internet.

For instance, some companies use websites to advertise their educational products. They usually say that their teaching method is better than any others.

Therefore, you need to develop special skills to research information on the internet.

Checkpoint

Do you know how to:

- find information on the internet?

- limit the amount of information you look at on the internet?

- check that the information on the internet is reliable?

If not, how can you learn these skills? _____

_____

_____

ACTIVITY 11.5

Time suggested:
As long as you need

Use written material to find information.

Use your own paper for this activity.

1 Use written material to find answers to some of the research questions that you developed in Activity 11.2.

2 Find:
- at least one example of hard copy
- at least one example of soft copy.

3 Make notes about the answers.

4 Discuss your notes with a friend.

Train your mind

1 Talk to different people about their ideas, and the reasons for their opinions.

2 Think about the reasons for *your* opinions.

3 Read often so that you develop good reading skills.

4 Practise using the library catalogue.

5 Practise finding information on the internet.

Summarise the chapter

Research is ...	
Reasons for researching	· · ·
Decide what you need to find out	Three reasons: · · ·
Make a list of research questions	Use: · ·
Choose only relevant information	
Be flexible	
Three methods	Oral communication · Friends and family · Classmates · Specialists · Public speakers Useful for: Disadvantages:
	Audio and audio-visual material · Audio · Audio-visual Useful for: Disadvantages:

	Written material
	· Hard copy
	· Soft copy
	Useful for:
	Disadvantages:

► Check your understanding

Choose the correct answers.

Check whether they are correct (page 286).

If they are not correct, read the information in this chapter again.

1 Planning and research should never be done at the same time. True or false?

2 When you learn:
    a you listen to someone talking or you read something
    b you understand and remember what you hear or see
    c you find a subject interesting and ask questions about it.

3 You are more likely to learn if you think carefully about something. True or false?

4 If you research information, you can use it to:
    a support what you write in your essay
    b show what you understand about learning styles
    c make your teacher very happy.

5 If you prepare some research questions before you start to look for information:
    a you will save time
    b you will save money
    c your reader will understand you more easily.

6 When you develop the research questions, you should not use the response questions. True or false?

7 When you use oral communication to find information:
    a you go to a public meeting and listen to a speaker
    b you talk and/or listen to other people
    c you use the telephone to have an interview.

8 Your teacher can check written material more easily than oral communication. True or false?

9 A radio programme is an example of audio-visual material. True or false?

10 Written material is often used for research because:
    a it can be soft or hard copy, and it is easy to find
    b it can be found on the internet, and it is often very complicated
    c it is a traditional source of information, and it can be checked easily.

12 Finding written material

Learning outcomes

When you have finished studying this chapter, you should be able to:

1. explain how to use keywords to search for written information;

2. find written information on the internet or an electronic database.

Use keywords to help you find relevant information.

What are keywords?

keywords important words about a subject

Keywords are important words about a subject.

> **They often appear in the essay question or the thesis statement or the response questions.**
>
> > Suppose that you were writing an essay about conservation. The thesis statement might be: Conservation is an individual responsibility. For this essay "conservation" is an important keyword.

> **Sometimes key words are not included in the essay question or the thesis statement. Then you have to think of them for yourself.**
>
> > For example, "recycle" is a word about conservation. It would be useful for the essay, but it does not appear in the thesis statement.

Why should you use keywords?

search engine a software program that uses keywords to find information that has been stored electronically

Keywords will help you to find useful information by using an internet search engine like Yahoo or Google. A search engine is a software program that uses your keywords to find information that has been stored electronically. Then it presents a list of items that contain those keywords. If you choose your keywords carefully, you are more likely to find useful information quickly. Most search engines offer both basic and advanced searches. It is a good idea to learn how to do an advanced search; different search engines use slightly different methods to plan a search.

Checkpoint

What search engines have you used? _____

What search engines do your friends use? _____

Keywords are useful when you are using an electronic database. It may be a library catalogue or a larger database service. They work in the same way as an internet search engine, but their searches are smaller.

> **electronic database** a software program that contains a collection of different publications

- A library catalogue is a database that contains only information about material that is held in that library.
- An electronic database service contains a collection of different written publications. For instance:
  - The Australian/New Zealand Reference Centre contains articles from magazines, newspapers and reference texts that are published in Australia and New Zealand. It is produced by EBSCO Information Service.
  - *Proquest 5000 International* is an American database that searches more than 10 000 magazines or journals

In addition, different electronic databases are suitable for finding information

Checkpoint

Which electronic databases are useful for the research that you need to do? _____

_____

_____

Are they available at the library that you use? _____

about different subjects.

Keywords will also help you think more clearly about the essay subject. As you think about which keywords might be useful, you will also think about what to include in your essay. As a result, you will gain a deeper understanding of the subject.

How do you decide which keywords to use?

You should have a flexible attitude when you are looking for information. If your search produces too many items, you must find ways to "narrow" or refine your search. If it produces too few items, you need to widen your search.

You should begin by looking at the work that you did when you started to plan.

> **You should look for important words in your analysis of the essay question, and in the thesis statement. It is also useful to look at the response questions.**
>
> > "Conservation" is the most obvious keyword in the example essay. "Individual responsibility" is also important. These two words should be used together (in a set) because they have a special meaning in this thesis statement. If you place them in quotation marks (" ..."), the search engine will look for where the same phrase appears in a publication.

> **If the keywords are too general, they will not be useful for your search.**
>
> > If you used "conservation" to look for information on the internet, you would find over 25 000 000 items*. It would be almost impossible to read all these items, or even to choose the most suitable ones. Even if you added "individual responsibility" as a second set of keywords, you would still find about 27 000 items.

> **Therefore, you should think of more precise keywords so that you can "narrow" or refine the search. You can do this by looking at:**
> - **your planning mind map**
> - **your free-writing**
> - **your essay outline.**
>
> > For example, you might decide to add "action" as a keyword. This would find 20 000 items which is still too large to manage.

ACTIVITY 12.1

Time suggested:
As long as you need

Identify some keywords.

You can do this activity on your own or with a friend. Use your own paper.

1   Choose an essay question. You can use the question that you used in Activities 11.2–11.5, or you can choose a new one.

2   Use the essay question, or the thesis statement and response questions, to identify some keywords.

3   Use the keywords to look for items on an internet search engine or electronic database.

4   Look at the work that you did during the planning stage. Use these ideas to identify some more keywords.

5   Use the new keywords to do another search.

6   If you worked alone, discuss your search with a friend.

---

*The statistics for the internet research examples were obtained by using Google in early 2005. Other search engines are likely to produce similar results.

You can add more keywords by looking at some of the items that you found.

Look at the first two or three pages of items that the search engine has found.

> Suppose that you found an item that included the words "reduce" and "re-use". This might remind you that "recycle" could be a useful keyword. These three words are more detailed than "conservation". They are also suitable for your search because they are about actions that individuals could do. You could ask the search engine to find items which include all of the words, or just some of them. This would give you more than 13 000 items.

You can limit your search in other ways.

You might ask for sources:
- **in a particular language**
- **from a particular period of time**
- **from a particular country.**

> You could ask for only items in English, or items that have been written during the past year. You could also ask only for New Zealand or Australian items. If you did this, you would find fewer items. This may still be quite a lot. However, it would be more manageable than the 25 000 000 that you found at the beginning of your search.

If you cannot find enough information, you must widen your search.

You can do this by truncating your keywords. This means that you shorten a keyword by deleting some letters and replacing them with a symbol. Many databases use an asterisk (*), but some use a question mark (?).The database looks for all the words that begin with the part of the word that you have not deleted.

> - You might truncate "conservation" to "conserv*". If you did this, the database would find "conserve" and "conserving" as well as "conservation".
> - If you truncated "responsibility" to "respons*', you would find "responsible", "response" and "responses". In this case, you might change the truncation to "responsib*" to find more relevant information.

truncate shorten a keyword by deleting some letters and replacing them with a symbol; used to widen a database search

You can also widen your search by deleting some of the keywords or by changing the limits.

> For example, you will find only one item if you:
> - use "conservation" and "individual responsibility" as keywords and
> - limit your search to New Zealand or Australian information from the past year.

ACTIVITY 12.2

Refine your search.

You can do this activity on your own or with a friend. Use your own paper.

1　Look at the first two or three pages of items that you found in Activity 12.1.
2　Read the titles and descriptions of each item.
3　Look for words that could be used as extra keywords.
4　Use these words to "narrow" your search.
5　Use truncation and add other limits if you need to widen your search.
6　Use the new keywords to do another search.
7　If you worked alone, discuss your search with a friend.

You should check whether the items are useful for your essay.

You can do this looking at the titles of the items, and their descriptions. Then you should think about whether they match your essay question, or the thesis statement and response questions.

For example, an item with a title like "Southern Islands Biodiversity Action Plan" is unlikely to be useful for your essay. However, you might decide to check an item that has information about "paper conservation".

You should also look for information about other relevant items.

You could click on:
• the links about similar pages, that the search engine supplies with each item.
• the information in an item about other useful websites.

ACTIVITY 12.3

Check whether items are useful for your essay, and find other useful items.

You can do this activity on your own or with a friend. Use your own paper.

1　Look at the first two or three pages of items that you found in Activity 12.2.
2　Read the titles and descriptions of each item.
3　If an item is likely to be useful for your essay, check whether it is suitable. (Click on the link and read it quickly.)
4　If it is useful, check the "similar pages" link that the search engine has provided.
5　Look for useful links inside the item itself.
6　If you worked alone, discuss what you did with a friend.

Train your mind

1　Practise thinking of keywords for different essay subjects.
2　Make sure that you can use the library catalogue.
3　Learn to use at least one internet search engine.
4　Learn to use at least one larger electronic database.

Summarise the chapter

Keywords	• Keywords are … • Uses
Use keywords to find information	• Internet search engine • Electronic database • Library catalogue
Choosing key words	From planning stage • • Refining during the search • • Widening your search • •

Finding other useful items	Two places to look
	•
	•

► Check your understanding

Choose the correct answers.

Check whether they are correct (page 286).

If they are not correct, read the information in this chapter again.

1 When you are researching, you can find all the information you need by using the first keywords that you think of. True or false?

2 You can start to develop keywords by looking at:
   a the library catalogue or a larger electronic database
   b your analysis of the essay question and/or the thesis statement
   c the introductory paragraph of your essay.

3 An electronic database contains a collection of information about different written publications. True or false?

4 Keywords are useful for:
   a using an internet search engine
   b using an electronic database
   c using a library catalogue
   d all of the above.

5 Once you have identified the keywords about a subject, you must not change them. True or false?

6 Your essay outline is:
   a not useful for helping you think of keywords
   b useful for helping you think of keywords
   c too general to be useful for your search.

7 You should always read every item that you find on the internet. True or false?

8 It is often a good idea to limit your search by asking for only recent information. True or false?

9 If you read the title and description of an item, you can often decide whether it is relevant for your essay. True or false?

10 If you click on the links that the search engine supplies about related websites:
   a you can often find extra relevant information
   b you will waste a lot of time reading useless information
   c you will get sore wrists from using the mouse too much.

13 Selecting and evaluating sources

Learning outcome

When you have finished studying this chapter, you should be able to:

1 Explain how to select and evaluate sources of information.

You should select your sources carefully.

What is a source?

source any 'place' where you find information or ideas

A source is any 'place' where you find information or ideas. It could be:

- a person
- a programme or tape
- a book or a chapter in a book
- an article in a newspaper or magazine
- a website or part of a website.

Checkpoint

Think about essays that you have written.

What sources did you use? _____

_____

_____

Why should you select your sources carefully?

There are three main reasons for selecting sources carefully.

- If your sources give wrong or misleading information, your essay will not be correct.
- If you choose information that is not at the right level for your essay, your explanations may be too simple or too complicated.
- If you cannot understand what you read or hear, you may choose information that is not relevant or useful for your essay.

How should you select sources of information?

evaluate examine something carefully and decide whether it is reliable and useful

You should evaluate every source of information that you find. This means that you should examine it carefully and decide whether it is likely to be reliable and useful. If you decide that it is not suitable for your essay, you should use a different source.

You should evaluate your sources carefully.

How should you evaluate a source?

You can evaluate a source by asking three general questions about it. Each question has several, more detailed questions that you can use. These questions are useful to evaluate any sort of source, whether it is oral, audio-visual or written. However, the examples in this chapter refer only to written material.

1   **Does the source contain useful information?**

This is the most important question to ask. If the information is not useful for your essay, you should not include it.

- **Does it help to answer at least one of the response questions in the essay outline?**

  If it does not do this, it is not useful.

  Suppose you were writing an essay with a thesis statement that said, "Conservation is an individual responsibility." Your response questions might be:
  - Why should people take personal responsibility for conservation?
  - Why is conservation not a government responsibility?

  For this essay, you would not use information about whether plastic is suitable for the windmills that generate electricity. However, you might be able to use information about recycling plastic bottles.

  You should remember to be flexible. The information in a source might suggest a response question that you have not thought of. In this case, you should use the source, after adding a response question to your essay outline.

  For example, you might find a source of information about how people can recycle or re-use plastic. You might decide to add a third response to the essay outline: "What can individual people do to help conservation?"

- **Is the information at the right level for the essay question?**

  If it is very simple, your essay will not have enough information.

  For example, the ideas in a primary school book will be too simple for your purpose. An article in a non-specialist magazine may include only very general information.

  You should use the marking schedule and your analysis of the essay question to help you decide whether to use the source.

- **Is there enough information?**

  If there is only a little information, it may be better to find a source with more details.

  > If a source includes only one idea about conservation, it may be better to find a different source. However, if there are a lot of details about that idea, it may be more useful than other, more general sources.

- **Is it up to date?**

  Generally, you should not use a source that is older than about five years. This is because ideas are changing all the time, as researchers discover new information.

  > For example, scientists are continually developing new ways of saving energy.

  However, you can use older sources if they are still relevant.

  > The Declaration of Human Rights was written in 1948. This is an older sources that could be used for an essay, because it is still important.

  Be careful about using sources that have no date. If you do not know when something was written, you do not know whether it is still correct. It is often difficult to find dates on websites.

ACTIVITY 13.1

Time suggested:
5–10 minutes

Check sources for usefulness.

Use the checklist on page 135, or use your own paper for this activity.

1   Look at the sources that you found in Activity 12.3, or use other sources of information that you have found.
2   Use the questions above to check whether these sources are useful.
3   Discuss your answers with a friend.

2   Is the source reliable?

If a source is reliable, it is more likely to contain information that is correct and up to date. You will lose marks if your essay contains incorrect information.

- **Is the author knowledgeable?**

  You should look for information about the author. Think about how much s/he is likely to know about the subject.

  > For example:
  > - A geology professor who specialises in oil exploration will know a lot about finding oil in New Zealand or Australia.
  > - A journalist or a politician is less likely to have this specialist knowledge.
  > - Someone writing in a chat room may have specialist knowledge, or may not.

Academic journals are often useful sources. They publish reports and articles (often called "papers") from people who have done research about specialist subjects.

For instance, *the New Zealand Journal of Ecology* and the *Australian Journal of Environmental Management* publish only information about ways to look after the environment in these countries.

Professional reports or magazines are also useful. Their writers and target readers are usually knowledgeable with special interest in their subjects.

For example, reports from the New Zealand Department of Conservation contain specialist information for people working in conservation in New Zealand. It also publishes a newsletter, *ConScience*, which has more general information.

You should be especially careful about information that you find on the internet. Anyone can publish information on the internet, even if they are not knowledgeable.

For instance, anyone can take part in a chat room, or develop a website.

- **Is the author likely to be unbiased?**

unbiased presenting both sides of an issue in a fair and balanced way

You should consider whether the author's opinions affect what s/he has written. Unbiased writers present opposing points of view in a fair and balanced way. They use words like "however" and "on the other hand" to acknowledge that there are different sides to an issue.

For example, someone who sells plastic bags is likely to advertise them as convenient and useful.

You should think about how a writer's opinions might have affected his or her writing.

The plastic bag seller is unlikely to include information about the environmental problems that plastic bags can cause. This writer is biased, so you would be very careful about using information from this source.

biased presenting only one point of view

If you use information only from a biased source, your essay will present only one point of view. If you include and explain opposing ideas, your essay will be more balanced.

ACTIVITY 13.2

Time suggested: 5–10 minutes

Check sources for reliability.

Use the checklist on page 135, or use your own paper for this activity.
1   Look at the sources that you used in Activity 13.1.
2   Use the questions above to check whether these sources are reliable.
3   Discuss your answers with a friend.

3   Is the information presented at the right level for you?

- **Is the layout easy to follow?**

  Whether you are reading a book, a chapter or a website, you should be able to find information easily. You should check:
  - the contents page
  - the introductory chapters
  - the title and introductory paragraph of a chapter or web page.

    For example, a chapter title like "The importance of recycling" gives clear information about what is in that chapter. However, a vague title, like "Around and around", would not help you to identify the contents quickly.

  You should check whether the headings and subheadings are useful and informative.

    If there are only a few headings, it will be harder to find information quickly.

  Diagrams, tables, graphs and other illustrations are also useful. They are often easier and quicker to understand than a paragraph containing only words.

    The examples in Figure 13.1 on page 134 contain the same information. Most people would find it quicker and easier to understand the table or the diagram than the paragraph.

Checkpoint

Look at Figure 13.1 on page 134. Which example is quickest and easiest for *you* to understand?

- **Can you understand the language?**

  Look at the vocabulary and the way the sentences are written. If you cannot understand them, you should look for another source.

    For example:
    - A text about conservation may contain specialist technical vocabulary, like "bio-diversity" or "environmental sustainability". If there are a lot of technical words, it will take you a long time to understand the information.
    - If the sentences are very long, they may be difficult to understand.

  If you can find an easier, reliable text, you will save time and understand the information better.

Conservation at home

There are many simple things that people can do at home to help conserve resources.

Firstly, they can reduce their use of electricity and water. They can save electricity by turning lights off when they leave a room. They can also avoid opening the refrigerator unnecessarily. Wearing warm clothes in winter will mean they need to use less heating. They can save water by having showers instead of baths and by repairing dripping taps. In addition, they should avoid using a 'running tap'. This means that they should use a plug in the sink when they wash dishes, and a bucket instead of a hose when they clean the car.

Secondly, they can re-use things so that they need to buy less. For example, they can wash plastic bags and glass jars after use, and use them again. They can also use newspaper for wrapping, and for cleaning windows.

Finally, they should recycle their rubbish. For instance, they can use organic household and garden waste to make compost. They should also place cans, glass, paper and plastics in a separate rubbish container for council recycling.

Reduce	Electricity	Turn off unneeded lights. Avoid opening refrigerator door. Wear warm clothes in winter.
	Water	Use showers instead of baths. Repair dripping taps. Avoid a 'running tap': – use the sink for washing dishes – use a bucket to wash the car.
Re-use	Wash and re-use	Plastic bags Glass jars
	Save and re-use	Newspaper (wrapping, cleaning windows)
Recycle	Make compost	Organic household and garden waste
	Separate rubbish for council	Cans Glass Paper

Figure 13.1   Information about conservation, presented in different ways

ACTIVITY 13.3   **Check whether sources are presented at the right level for you.**

Use the checklist below, or use your own paper for this activity.
1 Look at the sources you used in Activities 13.1 and 13.2.
2 Use the questions above to check whether these sources are at the right level for you.
3 Discuss your answers with a friend.

Time suggested:
5–10 minutes

Checklist

		✔ or ✗
1 Does the source contain useful information?	Does the information help to answer at least one of the response questions in the essay outline?	
	Is it at the right level for the essay question?	
	Is there enough information?	
	Is it up to date?	
2 Is the source reliable?	Is the author knowledgeable?	
	Is the author likely to be unbiased?	
3 Is the information presented at the right level for you?	Is the layout easy to follow?	
	Can you understand the language?	

Train your mind

1 Practise using the evaluation questions to decide whether you should believe what you hear and read.
2 Photocopy the checklist above so that you can practise using it.
3 Compare the sorts of information that you find from different sources.
4 Talk with your friends about which sources are useful and reliable.
5 Never write anything that you do not understand.

Summarise the chapter

Selecting sources	
A source is ...	
Reasons for choosing carefully	· · ·
Evaluating a source	**Does it contain useful information?** · · · ·
	Is it reliable? · ·
	Is the information at the right level? · ·

Check your understanding

Choose the correct answers.

Check whether they are correct (page 287).

If they are not correct, read the information in this chapter again.

1 A source is:
   a any 'place' where you find information
   b where you find information on an electronic database
   c the library in the place where you study.

2 You should be careful about using information from the internet because:
   a it could contain a virus
   b it might be unreliable
   c it is always wrong.

3 If you use irrelevant information, your essay will be off track. True or false?

4 If you use information that is very simple:
   a your essay may not have enough information
   b you will get good marks
   c your teacher will find it easy to understand.

5 When you evaluate a source of information, you must check how old the author is. True or false?

6 You should think about whether the author is likely to be biased, because:
   a you should use only biased information
   b you should never use biased information
   c you should present both sides of an issue.

7 When you check the layout of a source, you should think about:
   a whether the book looks attractive
   b whether the website was easy to find
   c whether you can find information easily.

8 If the chapter title is funny or unusual, it is easier to understand. True or false?

9 Diagrams and tables:
   a are more interesting than words
   b are often easier to understand quickly
   c use a lot more space than words.

10 If you do not understand what you read, you should copy it into your essay because it will sound good. True or false?

14 Recording references

Learning outcomes

When you have finished studying this chapter, you should be able to:

1. explain why it is important to record references;
2. explain the principles of recording references;
3. use the Harvard or APA system to write a list of references or a bibliography.

Referencing is an important part of academic writing.

What is referencing?

referencing recording your sources of information

text written information

Harvard system a method of recording references, developed by Harvard University; sometimes called "author-date" or "name-year" system

APA system a method of recording references, developed by the American Psychological Association

You use referencing to record your sources, that is, the 'places' where you found information. Usually your sources will be texts (written information) that someone else has written. It is a good idea to write down the references when you are doing research. This saves time later if you need to re-check a source, and when you are making a list of references.

There are many different ways of ways of recording references. Most universities and polytechnics in New Zealand and Australia use either the Harvard system or the APA system.

- The Harvard system is sometimes called the 'author-date' or the 'name-year' system. It was developed at Harvard University at the end of the 19th century.
- The APA system was developed by the American Psychological Association.

The Harvard and APA systems use the same basic principles, but they have slightly different ways of recording the details. This chapter gives examples of both systems. It includes the information that you are most likely to need for referencing academic essays.

Checkpoint

Which referencing system do *you* need to use? _____

_____

Why do you need to use referencing?

Referencing helps you demonstrate your research skills. When you use referencing, you show how well you can find and select information that other people have written.

You can also use referencing to support your ideas. Your teachers are more likely to believe what you write if you can show that someone else agrees with you. (See Chapter 11, page 110, for more information about this.)

You can use referencing in two ways.

- You can make a list of references. This includes all the sources of information you used in your essay. It does not include everything that you read. This sort of list is most useful for certificate and undergraduate writing.

- You can make a bibliography. This is a list of all the sources of information that you found about a subject. It is useful if the reader wants to find a lot of information about a subject. Bibliographies are usually used for advanced undergraduate or postgraduate writing.

list of references a list of the sources of information that you used in an essay

bibliography a list of all the sources of information that you found about a subject

Checkpoint

Will you need to write lists of references or bibliographies for your essays? _____

_____

Accurate referencing protects you against plagiarism.

What is plagiarism?

Plagiarism happens when you present other people's ideas or words as if they were your own. It is a bit like stealing. Instead of stealing things, the writer steals another person's thoughts or writing. Plagiarism happens if you:

- use someone else's ideas without saying where you found them (without acknowledging them)

- copy phrases or sentences from a book or other printed material (including other students' essays) without acknowledgement

- copy from the internet without acknowledgement.

plagiarism presenting other people's ideas or words as if they were your own

acknowledgement a statement about where you found information or an idea

Sometimes, students copy without meaning to. They may find it easier than writing their own words. They may think that they cannot explain something as well as the author does.

Plagiarism is treated seriously in universities and polytechnics. If you plagiarise, you may be given no marks, or you may be told to leave a course. In the past, it has been difficult to discover whether a student has been plagiarising. However, many teachers are now using the internet to check students' work. It is becoming easier for them to discover whether your work is original or copied. If you want to do well in your studies, it is very important to avoid plagiarism.

How can you avoid plagiarism?

There are three things that you can do to avoid plagiarism:

1   Write a complete list of references that includes every source of information that you have used to support your writing. The information in this chapter will help you do this.

2   Use citations in your essay, to show where you found each piece of information. See Chapter 19 for information about citations (pages 201–212).

3   Use your own words as much as possible. Chapter 16, pages 168–171, has useful information about this.

Recording references is not difficult if you use the ICU formula.

What is the ICU formula?

> **ICU formula** three steps for recording a reference; includes identifying the sort of publication, checking the information needed and using the correct format

ICU is a mnemonic to help you remember the three steps for recording references. The three steps are:

Step 1 Identify the sort of publication.

Step 2 Check that you have all the information that you need.

Step 3 Use the correct format.

A diagram of the ICU formula is cyclical, a bit like the writing process model in Chapter 4 (see page 45).

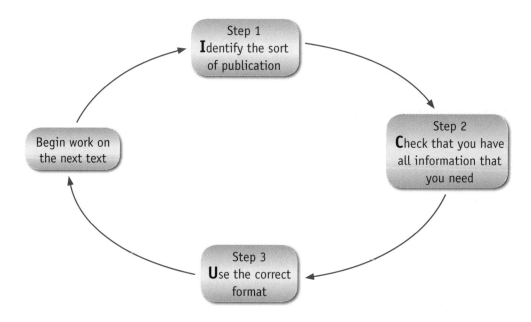

Figure 14.1 The ICU formula

Important vocabulary for recording references

ampersand a symbol that means "and", written &

colon a symbol that separates pieces of information, written:

edition a reprinted version of a book, with changes from the first printing

editor a person who organises people working together to produce a book

issue number a number that shows when a particular journal edition was published in a year

italics *sloping writing*

lower case small letters, e.g. a, b, c

retrieval details information about the database or website that you used to find a text

upper case capital letters, e.g. A, B, C

volume number a number that shows the year that a particular journal edition was published

How do you use the ICU formula to record references?

The ICU formula is described below. As you read the explanations, look carefully at the examples.

Situation

Imagine that you are writing an essay about the effects of energy drinks on sports performance. During your research, you found eight texts containing useful information. You have checked that they are reliable and up to date. Now you need to record the references.

There will be eight items in your list of references. You must use the correct referencing format for each item.

The Harvard system has several versions

There is no specific manual for the Harvard system. Many universities publish guidelines on their websites, but they often use different formats. The main differences are in using punctuation and brackets. Different guidelines have different rules about:

- whether to use full stops after the authors' initials
- whether to place the year of publication in brackets
- whether to use full stops or commas between each part of a reference item.

The examples in this chapter have been developed from the guidelines published by Flinders University, Monash University and the University of South Australia. However, when you use the Harvard system, you should use the guidelines published by your university or polytechnic.

To record a reference for a book

Step 1 Identify the sort of publication.

One of the texts is a **book** called *Exercise Physiology: Energy, Nutrition, and Human Performance*.

Step 2 Check that you have all the information that you need.

You need five details:

- the family name and initials of the **author**
- the **year the book was published**
- the **title** of the book
- an **edition number** (if there is one). An edition is a reprinted version of a book. A second edition includes changes from the first printing, perhaps because of new information or ideas. The first edition of a book does not usually have a number.
- **publishing information** – the city of publication and the publisher.

The **authors** are William D. McArdle, F.I. Katch and V.L. Katch. The book was published in **2001**. The **title** is *Exercise Physiology: Energy, Nutrition, and Human Performance*. The book is a fifth **edition**. It was **published** in Philadelphia by Lippincott Williams and Williams.

Step 3 Use the correct format.

Harvard format

- Place the family names of the **authors** before their initials. If there are several authors:
  - use commas to separate them
  - use an ampersand (&) between the last two
  - do not use a comma before the ampersand.
- Wrap the **publishing year** in brackets (depending on the Harvard version that you are using).
- Record the **title** of the book.
  - Use italics *(sloping print)* if it is typed; underline it if it is handwritten.
  - Use upper case to begin the first word of the title, and lower case to begin the other words. An upper case letter is a capital letter, for example A or B or C. A lower case letter is a small letter, like a or b or c. Always use upper case to begin names of places and people, for example, **A**ustralia, **N**ew **Z**ealand, **W**iti Ihimaera, **D**avid Malouf.
  - If the title has two parts, separate them with a colon (:), and begin each part with upper case.
  - Place a comma after the title.
- If there is an **edition number**, add it after the title, followed by a comma. The word "edition" can be written as "ed" or "edn" (depending on the Harvard version).
- Add the **publishing details**. Place a comma between the publisher's name and the city of publication. You do not need to include the name of the country if the book was published in:
  - an important and well-known city, like London or Paris (or Philadelphia).
  - America. If the city is not well known, add the short form of the state, for example IL for Illinois or MD for Maryland.
- Finish with a full stop.

Harvard format for this text is:

McArdle, W.D., Katch, F.I. & Katch, V.L. (2001) *Exercise physiology: Energy, nutrition, and human performance*, 5th ed, Lippincott Williams & Wilkins, Philadelphia.

APA format

- Place the family names of the **authors** before their initials. If there are several authors:
  - use commas to separate them
  - place an ampersand (&) between the last two.
- Wrap the **publishing year** in brackets.
- Record the **title** of the book.
  - Use italics *(sloping print)* if it is typed; underline it if it is handwritten.
  - Use upper case to begin the first word of the title, and lower case to begin the other words.
  - If the title has two parts, separate them with a colon (:), and begin each part with upper case. Use upper case to begin names of places and people.
- If the book has an **edition number**, add it in brackets after the title. Abbreviate the word "edition" (ed.).
- Add the **publishing details**. Place a colon between the place of publication and the publisher's name. You do not need to include the name of the country if the book was published in:
  - an important and well-known city, like London or Paris (or Philadelphia)
  - America. If the city is not well known, add the short form of the name of the state, for example, IL for Illinois or MD for Maryland.
- **Separate each set of details** with a full stop.

APA format for this text is:

McArdle, W.D., Katch, F.I., & Katch, V.L. (2001). *Exercise physiology: Energy, nutrition and human performance* (5th ed.). Philadelphia: Lippincott Williams & Wilkins.

Checkpoint

Check each detail of the example for the system that you need to use.

Identifying family and personal names

You must be able to identify family and personal names when you use the APA and Harvard systems for referencing. Different cultures have different ways of using people's names. Western cultures generally place personal names before the family name. This can be a problem for people from other cultures with different traditions.

- If a book is printed in English, the name of the author is usually presented with the personal name or initials before the family name. For example: Thomas Keneally, James K. Baxter and C. K. Stead are well-known writers.
  - Thomas Keneally's personal name is Thomas; its initial is T. His family name is Keneally.
  - James K. Baxter used a name and an initial for his personal names: James and K. The initials for both these personal names are J. K. His family name is Baxter.
  - C. K. Stead uses initials for his personal names. His family name is Stead.
- Generally, newspapers, magazines and journals list writers' names in the same way as books do.
- Electronic databases and websites use several different ways to list writers' names.
  - Sometimes the family name is printed in uppercase (capital letters). It may be placed before or after the personal name. For example, you might find "WRIGHT Judith" or "Judith WRIGHT" at the top of an article or paper. Wright is the family name. Judith is her personal name; its initial is J.
  - Sometimes the family name is printed first, and separated from the personal name by a comma. The family name may or may not be printed in uppercase. For example, you might find "Sharples, Pita" or "SHARPLES, Pita". Sharples is his family name. His personal name is Pita. The initial for his personal name is P.

ACTIVITY 14.1

Record references for books.

1   Find two books. You can use sources from the activities in Chapter 13 (pages 129–137), or find different ones.

2   Record the references for each one. Use Harvard or APA format.

3   Check your answers with a friend.

Time suggested:
As long as you need

_____

_____

_____

_____

To record a reference for a chapter in a book

Step 1 Identify the sort of publication.

One of the texts is a **chapter in a book**. The rest of the book is not relevant for your essay.

Step 2 Check that you have all the information that you need.
As well as the **information for a whole book**, you need:
· the **author of the chapter**
· the **title of the chapter**
· the **page numbers**
· the name of the book's **editor** (or editors). An editor is a person who organises people working together to produce a book. Each person may write one chapter or several.

The **author of the chapter** is L.L.Spriet and the **chapter title** is "Caffeine". The **book title** is *Performance-enhancing substances in sport and exercise*. The **editors** are M.S.Bahrke and C.E.Yesalis. The book was **published** in 2002 by a company called Human Kinetics in Champaign, Illinois, USA. The chapter is on **pages** 267–278.

Step 3 Use the correct format.
Use the same general format as for a whole book. Add information about the chapter before the information about the book.

Harvard format
· Place the **author of the chapter** at the beginning.
  – Put the family name before the initials.
  – Use commas and an ampersand (&) if necessary.
· Place the publishing **year** after the author.
· Put the **chapter title** after the year. Use a regular font (not italics or underlined). Add a comma.
· Write "**in**" to show that the item is a part of a book. Add a colon (:).
· Add the **editor's family name and initials**, followed by "**(ed)**". Use an ampersand and "**(eds)**" if necessary.
· Write the **title of the book**, using italics (or underline it). Add a comma (,).
· Add the **publishing information**, then a comma.
· Add the **page numbers** at the end. Use "p." for a single page and "pp." for more than one. Use a hyphen (-) between page numbers.
· Finish with a full stop.

Harvard format for this chapter is:
Spriet, L.L. (2002) Caffeine, in: Bahrke, M.S. and Yesalis, C.E. (eds) *Performance-enhancing substances in sport and exercise*, Human Kinetics, Champaign, IL, pp.267–278.

APA format
· Place the **author of the chapter** at the beginning.
  – Put the family name before the initials.
  – Use commas and an ampersand (&) if necessary.
· Place the publishing **year** in brackets after the author. Add a full stop.
· Put the **chapter title** after the **year**. Use a regular font (not italics or underlined). Add a full stop.
· Write "**In**" to show that the chapter is part of a book.
· Add the **editor's name** with the initials before the family name. *This is different from the usual order for a book.*
  – Use commas and an ampersand if necessary.
  – Do not use a comma before the ampersand.
  – Place (**Ed.**) or (**Eds.**) after the editor's name, and add a full stop.
· Use italics (or underlining) for the **book title**.
· Add the **page numbers** in brackets immediately after the book title. Use "p." for a single page and "pp." for more than one. Use a hyphen (-) between page numbers.
· Add the **publishing information** at the end.
· Finish with a full stop.

APA format for this text is:
Spriet, L.L. (2002). Caffeine. In M.S.Bahrke & C.E.Yesalis (Eds.), *Performance-enhancing substances in sport and exercise* (pp. 267–278). Champaign, IL: Human Kinetics.

Checkpoint

Check each detail of the example for the system that you need to use.

ACTIVITY 14.2   **Record references for chapters in books.**

1   Find two books with chapters written by different people.
2   Record the references for one chapter from each book. Use Harvard or APA format.
3   Check your answers with a friend.

Time suggested:
As long as you need

_____

_____

_____

_____

Checkpoint

Read the table below and check each detail of the example for the system that you need to use.

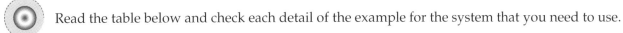

To record references for newspaper and magazine articles

Step 1 Identify the sort of publication.
 · Newspapers are usually published daily or weekly. They report information about local, national or international events. They usually aim for a general readership.
 · Magazines are published weekly or monthly, or sometimes less often. They publish articles to interest specific target readers. However, the articles may be about different subjects. For instance:
   – the articles in a golf magazine could be about any aspect of golf: golf personalities, golf competitions, golfing equipment, tips to help people play better
   – the articles in a magazine for business managers might be about managing people, changes in tax laws, or interviewing possible employees.
 You have found two articles, one in the *Sunday Star-Times* **newspaper** and one in *Consumer* **magazine**.

Step 2 Check that you have all the information that you need.   You need: · the family name and initials of the **author**   · the exact **date of publication** (not just the year)   · the **title of the article**   · the **page number(s)**   · the **name of the newspaper or magazine**.   The **newspaper article is called** "Drinks in a fix over caffeine". It was **written by** A. Richardson and it appeared on **page** A3 of the *Sunday Star-Times* on **12 May 2002**.   The **magazine article** was printed on **page 14** of *Consumer* in **May 2002**. (*Consumer* is a monthly magazine, so there is no number for the day.) The **article is called** "The truth about 'energy' drinks". There is **no information about the author**.

Step 3 Use the correct format.
If you know the author's name, you can record the reference in a straightforward way.

Harvard format
- List the **author(s)** first, surname followed by initials. Use commas and an ampersand (&) if necessary.
- Put the **year** in brackets.
- Write the **title** of the article, wrapped in single quotation marks and followed by a comma. Use upper case to begin the first word, and lower case to begin other words.
- Add the **name of the newspaper** in italics (or underline it). Use upper case to begin all the important words. (Copy from the newspaper or magazine.) Follow with a comma.
- Add the **day and month** and a comma.
- Add the **page number(s)** and a full stop.

Harvard format for this newspaper article is:
Richardson, A. (2002) 'Drinks in a fix over caffeine', *Sunday Star-Times*, 12 May, p. A3.

APA format
- List the **author(s)** first, surname followed by initials. Use commas and an ampersand (&) if necessary.
- Put the **year, month and day** in brackets, with a comma after the year.
- Use a regular font for the **title of the article** (not italics or underlined). Use upper case to begin the first word, and lower case for the other words.
- Use italics (or underlining) for the **name of the newspaper or magazine**. Place it after the name of the article. Use upper case to begin all the important words in the title. (Copy from the newspaper or magazine.)
- Add a comma and the **page number** at the end.
- Take special care with punctuation (commas and full stops).

APA format for this newspaper article is:
Richardson, A. (2002, May 12). Drinks in a fix over caffeine. *Sunday Star-Times*, p. A3.

If you do not know the author's name, you have to make some changes.

Harvard format
- Place the **title of the article**, in single quotation marks, at the beginning.
- Add the **year** in brackets.
- Add the **name of the magazine or newspaper** in italics. Follow with a comma.
- Write the **day and month** and follow with a comma. (In this example, the day is not available because the magazine is published monthly.)
- Add the **page number** and finish with a full stop.

Harvard format for this magazine article is:
'The truth about "energy" drinks' (2002) *Consumer*, May, p. 14.

APA format
- Place the **title of the article** at the beginning of the record, before the **date**.
- Place the **name of the newspaper or magazine** and the **page number(s)** after the date.

APA format for this magazine article is:
The truth about "energy" drinks. (2002, May). *Consumer*, p.14.

ACTIVITY 14.3   **Record references for newspapers and magazines.**

Time suggested:
As long as you need

1   Find two articles from a newspaper or a magazine:
- one which includes the author's name
- one where the author is not known.

2   Record the references for each one. Use APA or Harvard format.

3   Check your answers with a friend.

_____

_____

_____

_____

To record references for articles or papers in a journal

Step 1 Identify the sort of publication.

- Journals publish information about specific topics for specific groups of readers. Academic journals are usually concerned with papers (reports) about research. For example, the *Communication Journal of New Zealand* prints research papers about communication. Most of its readers are teachers and researchers of communication studies.
- Professional journals publish articles that will interest readers in specific career areas. For example, the *National Business Review* publishes articles about business. Most of its readers are business people in New Zealand.

You have found one **article in a journal**.

Step 2 Check that you have all the information that you need.

You need:
- the family name and initials of the **author**
- the **title of the paper or article**
- the **name of the journal**
- the **year** of publication
- the **volume and issue numbers**
  - A volume number shows the year that a particular edition was published.
  - An issue number shows when a particular edition was published during that year. If only one edition is printed in a year, there will be no issue number.
  - For example, "volume 5, issue 3" would be the third edition to be published in the fifth year after the journal was first printed.
- **page number(s).**

The **author** is E. Ban. The **title of the article** is "Sports, energy and cordial market: Growth spurt for energy drinks". It was **published in** *Retail World* in **2002**. The **volume number** is 55; the **issue number** is 19. This is a one-page article; it is printed on **page** 26.

Step 3 Use the correct format.

The format is very similar to a newspaper article. However, the volume, issue and page numbers must be included.

Harvard format
- Write the **author's name**, family name followed by initials. Use commas and an ampersand (&) if necessary.
- Add the **year** in brackets.
- Write the **title of the article**.
  - Use a regular font (not italics or underlined).
  - Wrap in single quotation marks.
  - Follow with a comma.
- Add the **name of the journal** in italics (or underline it)
  - Use upper case to begin all the important words in the journal name. (Copy from the journal.)
  - Add a comma.
- Add the **volume number** using "vol.", then add another comma.
- Place the **issue number** next, using "no.".
- Add the **page number(s)**, using "p." or "pp.". Finish with a full stop.

Harvard format for this article is: Ban, E. (2002) 'Sports energy and cordial market: Growth spurt for energy drinks', *Retail World*, vol. 55, no. 19, p. 26.

APA format
- List the **author(s)** first, family name followed by initials. Use commas and an ampersand (&) if necessary.
- Add the **year** in brackets.
- Add the **title of the article** or paper
  - Use a regular font (not italics or underlined).
  - Use upper case to begin the first word only.
- Place the **name of the journal** next.
  - Use italics (or underline it).
  - Use upper case to begin all the important words in the journal name. (Copy from the journal.)
  - Add a comma.
- Add the **volume number**. Use italics (or underline it).
- Place the **issue number** in brackets next to the volume number.
  - Do not leave any space between the volume and issue numbers.
  - Add a comma.
- Write the **page number(s)**.
- Finish with a full stop.

APA format for this article is: Ban, E. (2002). Sports, energy and cordial market: Growth spurt for energy drinks. *Retail World, 55*(19), 26.

Checkpoint

Check each detail of the example for the system that you need to use.

ACTIVITY 14.4

Time suggested:
As long as you need

Record references for journal articles or papers.

1   Find two articles or papers from journals. If possible, use:
  • one from a professional journal
  • one from an academic journal.
2   Record the references for each one. Use APA or Harvard format.
3   Check your answers with a friend.

_____

_____

_____

_____

To record references from an electronic database (APA format)

Step 1 Identify the sort of publication.

If you are using the APA system and you find information in a database, you must add the retrieval details. This is information about where and when you found the text.

You found the journal article (see example above) in an **electronic database.**

Step 2 Check that you have all the information that you need.
As well as the **information about the text**, you need:
• the **name of the database**
• the **date that you retrieved** (found) the text.
You used the *Proquest 5000 International* **database** on **5 August 2006.**

Step 3 Use the correct format.
After you have recorded the reference for the text, add details about the database.
•   Write "**Retrieved**".
•   Add the **date that you found the information**, with the month and day, a comma and the year.
•   Write "**from**" and the **name of the database.**

APA format for this article is: Ban, E. (2002). Sports, energy and cordial market: Growth spurt for energy drinks. *Retail World*, *55*(19), 26. Retrieved August 5, 2006 from *Proquest 5000 International* database.

Checkpoint

Check each detail of the example if you need to use APA format.

ACTIVITY 14.5   **Record retrieval details for an electronic database (APA format only).**

1   Find two journal articles or papers in an electronic database.
2   Record the references and retrieval details for each one.
3   Check your answers with a friend.

Time suggested:
As long as you need

To record references from the internet

Step 1 Identify the sort of publication.

If you find information on a website, you must add the retrieval details to the reference record. This is information about where and when you found the text.

You have found three relevant and up-to-date **texts on the internet**.

Step 2 Check that you have all the information that you need.

Websites are often difficult to record. You must look carefully to find as many details as possible.
· The **URL** (internet address) of the website is the most important piece of information.
· The **author(s)** may not be listed, or they may be hard to find.
· Sometimes there is no **date of publication**, so you do not know whether or not the text is up to date.
· You must record the **date of retrieval**.
· The *Science Daily* **website** has an **article** called "Combining energy drinks with alcohol potentially dangerous". It was **originally published in 2001** in a **journal** called *Science Daily*. The URL is http://www.sciencedaily. com/releases/2001/11/011116065754.You **found it** on 2 August 2006.
· You have found a **website** with an article called "Sports energy drinks". The **copyright date** at the bottom of the page is 2001. You **found it** on 4 August 2006. The **URL** is http://mama.essortment.com/information_rmus.htm
· **You** have found a **website** called *Smartplay*. It has an **article** called "The buzz on energy drinks". You **retrieved it** on 1 August 2006 but you could not find a publication date. The **URL** is http://www.smartplay.net/whatsnew/whatsnew.html

Step 3 Use the correct format

Harvard format
· If possible, list the **author** first. This might be a company or group of people.
· If there is no author, place the **title of the text** first.
· If there is **no publication date**, use (n.d.). "n.d." stands for "no date".
· List the **title of the text** (use italics or underline if the text is not part of a larger website).
· If the text is part of a larger website, you can list the **website** in italics. (That is, treat the text like a newspaper article.)
· Write "Available:" and add the **URL**.
· Use brackets and "Accessed:" to show the **retrieval date**. Finish with a full stop.

APA format
· List the **author** first. This might be a company or group of people.
· If there is no author, place the **title of the text** first.
· If there is no **publication date**, use (n.d.). "n.d." stands for "no date".
· List the **title of the text** (use italics or underline if the text is not part of a larger website).
· If the text is part of a larger website, you can list the **website** in italics. (That is, treat the text like a newspaper article.)
· Add the **retrieval date**.
· Include the **URL**.

▶

Harvard format for these articles is:

'Combining energy drinks with alcohol potentially dangerous' (2001) *Science Daily*, Available: http://www.sciencedaily.com/releases/2001/11/011116065754.htm (Accessed: 2006, August 2).

'Sports energy drinks' (2001), Available: http://mama.essortment.com/information_rmus.htm (Accessed: 2006, August 4).

'The buzz on energy drinks', (n.d.) *Smartplay*. Available: http://www.smartplay.net/whatsnew/whatsnew.html (Accessed: 2006, August 1).

APA format for these articles is:

Combining energy drinks with alcohol potentially dangerous. (2001). *Science Daily*. Retrieved August 2, 2006, from Science Daily website: http://www.sciencedaily.com/releases/2001/11/011116065754.htm

Sports energy drinks. (2001). Retrieved August 4, 2006, from: http://mama.essortment.com/information_rmus.htm

The buzz on energy drinks. (n.d.). *Smartplay*. Retrieved August 1, 2006, from the Smartplay website: http://www.smartplay.net/whatsnew/whatsnew.html

Checkpoint

Check each detail of the examples for the system that you need to use.

ACTIVITY 14.6

Time suggested: As long as you need

Record references from the internet.

1   Find two pieces of information from the internet.
2   Record the references and retrieval details for each one. Use APA or Harvard format.
3   Check your answers with a friend.

_____

_____

_____

_____

You must present the list of references correctly.

How should you present the list of references?

The list of references should be printed or written at the end of the essay. It is an important part of the essay so you should spend time on making sure that it is correct. Figures 14.2 and 14.3 show you how to do this (see page 151).

Generally APA and Harvard have identical rules about the presentation. They both:

- use alphabetical order
- leave an empty line between each entry
- indent second and following lines for each item. (This means that they leave about five blank spaces at the beginning of every line except the first one.)

However, you should remember that there are several different versions of the Harvard system; use whichever version is required at your institution.

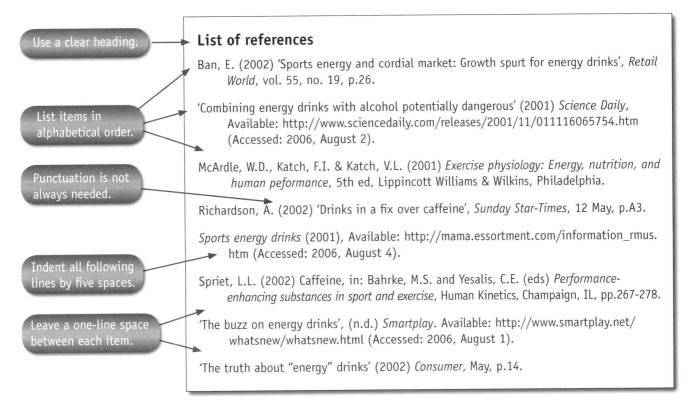

Figure 14.2 Example of a list of references: Harvard format

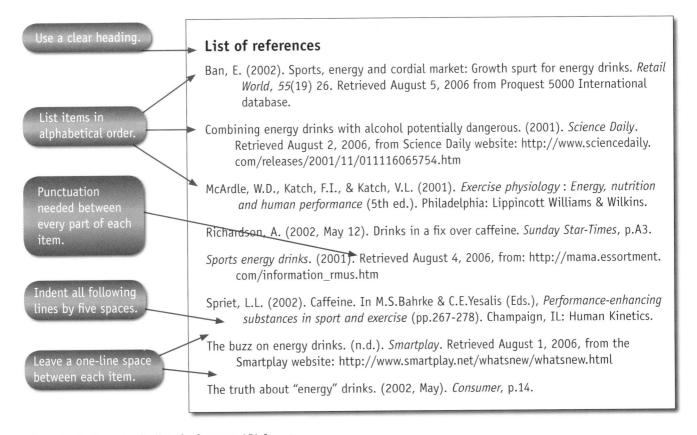

Figure 14.3 Example of a list of references: APA format

Train your mind

1   Make sure that you avoid plagiarising.
2   Practise identifying different sorts of publication.
3   Practise using the ICU formula.
4   Practise recording references.
5   If you are not sure how to record something, use this chapter to help you.

Summarise the chapter

Referencing is ...	
Reasons for recording references	• •
Ways to use references	• •
Referencing systems	• •
Plagiarism	What it is: • • • How to avoid plagiarising • • •
The ICU formula	(Explain each step or draw a diagram)

Recording references (Make notes about the system that you must use)	**Books** • Author • Publishing year • Title • Edition number • Publishing information • Punctuation
	Chapters in books **Same details as for books, and** • Author of chapter • Title of chapter • Page numbers • Editor's name

	Newspaper and magazine articles
	 • Author of article
	   – if known
	   – if unknown
	 • Date of publication
	 • Title of article
	 • Name of newspaper or magazine
	 • Page number
	 • Punctuation

	Articles or papers in journals • Author • Year of publication • Title of article or paper • Name of journal • Volume number • Issue number • Page numbers • Punctuation

Electronic databases (APA format only)

· Name of database

· Date retrieved

The internet

· Author

· Year of publication

· Date of retrieval

· URL

Check your understanding

Choose the correct answers.

Check whether they are correct (page 287).

If they are not correct, read the information in this chapter again.

1 If you record references during the research stage, you will save time later on. True or false?

2 If you use other people's ideas or words, and put them in your essay:
   a you will always lose marks
   b you must record a reference
   c you will always get full marks.

3 There is no difference between the Harvard and APA systems of referencing. True or false?

4 You can use the ICU formula to help you record references. ICU stands for:
   a **I**talicising the author's name, **C**opying all the details, **U**nderstanding the ideas
   b **I**ndenting the second line, **C**hecking the information, **U**sing the correct format
   c **I**dentifying the sort of publication, **C**hecking the information, **U**sing the correct format.

5 When you record a reference, you should always check the punctuation carefully. True or false?

6 When you record a reference for a whole book, you must place the author's family name after the personal initials. True or false?

7 When you record the reference for a chapter in a book, you must include:
   a the number of the chapter
   b the page numbers
   c only the title of the chapter.

8 When you use APA format, "ed." and "Ed." mean the same thing. True or false?

9 When you record references for an article from a newspaper or magazine, you must:

   a include as much of the publication date as possible

   b include the day and month of publication

   c include the month of publication

   d include only the year of publication.

10 When you record references from a journal, you must always include the page number. True or false?

If you need more details ...

This chapter explains only basic information about the Harvard and APA systems.

    If you need more information about the Harvard system, you should use the guidelines published by your university or polytechnic. (There is no specific manual for the Harvard system.)

    If you need more details about the APA system, you can look at the publication manual of the American Psychological Association. The Purdue University website also has very clear guidelines about APA. Its URL is: http://owl.english.purdue.edu/handouts/print/research/r_apa.html (Retrieved May 1, 2005)

15 Reading for research

When you have finished studying this chapter, you should be able to:

1 Explain the purpose of research reading;

2 Describe and use some strategies for effective research reading.

You should develop special strategies for effective research reading.

What is a strategy?

A strategy is a way of planning how to do something. The way that you read when you are researching will affect the amount of information you can find. It will also affect the quality of your essay.

Why should you develop special reading strategies?

Reading for research is more than just looking at words. When you are researching information, your main purpose is to find information that will be useful for your essay.

- You usually want to work quickly because you have to complete the essay and hand it in on time.
- You must find information that is correct, up to date and relevant for your essay.
- You need to make notes about details and examples as well as about general ideas.

This is quite different from other sorts of reading, like reading for pleasure or reading to revise for an examination.

What strategies should you use?

You should develop your research questions and keywords before you begin to read. If you do this, it will be easier to find relevant information. Think about:

- what you need to know
- what your target reader needs to know.

When you find a text, you should scan it and then skim read.

Scan it first to see whether it is likely to contain useful information. When you scan, you do not read a whole text. Instead you look at important parts that can tell you whether the text is worth reading more carefully.

- If the text is a whole book, look at the contents page and check the chapter titles.
- Look at the headings and sub-headings.
- Look at the diagrams and tables and decide if they are relevant to the subject you are writing about.

> **scan** look quickly at important parts of a text to see if it is likely to contain useful information

Suppose that you are writing an essay about public transport in your town. When you search for information, you find a report from the local council. The report is called "A study of the current bus and coach services in _____ town". You could scan the contents and the headings to decide whether the report contains useful information for your essay. It the information is not useful, you should look for another text.

If the text looks useful, skim it to find information that will help to answer your research questions. Skimming involves reading very fast. You do not always need to read all the words, just the important ones.

- Check whether the writer has placed the topic sentences consistently (always in the same place). They should be at the beginning or the end of the paragraphs. If s/he has done this, you can understand the general meaning by reading the topic sentences.
- Look for keywords that you identified when you began your research.

> **skim** read very fast, reading only the important words

Skimming the relevant sections of the report might tell you that there are problems with the bus routes. You might also discover that the writer of the report thinks that the council should build a new bus station.

Skimming is suitable for finding general ideas, not details.

ACTIVITY 15.1   **Scan and skim a text.**

Time suggested:
10–15 minutes

1   Scan this textbook to find information about research questions and keywords. (They are in different chapters.)
- Scan the contents page to find the relevant chapters.
- Scan the chapters to find the information.
2   Skim the paragraphs so that you get a general understanding of the information.
- Look for topic sentences and key words.
- Do not read every word.
3   Explain to a friend what you did.

Sometimes you need to read carefully.

Maybe the information or ideas are complicated or difficult to understand. Maybe you need to find details or examples for your essay. In these situations, skimming and scanning is not enough.

For the public transport example, you might need to know which bus routes have problems. You might need to find out why the writer wants the council to build a new bus station. Therefore, you need to read the report more thoroughly.

It is a good idea to read the text several times. Begin by reading quickly, without checking words that you do not understand. At this stage, your purpose is to have a general understanding of the information. You will usually understand more information each time that you read the text. You do not need to know the exact meaning of every word.

Suppose that there is some difficult vocabulary in the report section about replacing the bus station. One sentence might say, "The current dilapidated state of the superstructure greatly endangers the general public and urgent replacement is imperative." However, other sentences explain that there are holes in the roof and some of the concrete pillars are dangerous.

Once you have a general understanding of the text, you can identify the most important ideas. If you cannot understand the general meaning of the text, you may need to use your dictionary. However, you should do this only if you really cannot understand the main ideas, or if you really need to understand an important detail. Otherwise, using the dictionary just makes your reading slower.

If you understand the main problems about the bus station, you do not need to check the meanings of the unfamiliar words.

This sort of reading will usually find the information that you need to support your essay.

Checkpoint

How much detailed information will you need for your essays?

Will you need a general understanding, or a lot of complicated detail? _____

_____

Develop your reading skills

Reading is a skill that improves with practice and persistence. It is a good idea to work on improving your reading speed. Count how many words you can read over, say, one minute, then try to beat your 'record'. It doesn't matter if you don't understand every word. If you practise every day, you will learn to read faster.

ACTIVITY 15.2

Time suggested:
10–15 minutes
(after finding the text)

Read a text for general understanding.

1 Find a text that has information to support an essay that you are going to write. You can use a text from the activities in Chapter 14, or you can use a different one.

2 Use the reading strategies described above to get a general understanding of the text.
   • Read the text quickly several times.
   • Do not use a dictionary.
   • Think about whether you have a general understanding of the text.

3 Explain the main ideas to a friend.

You should think critically about what you read.

Research reading should be a thoughtful and questioning activity. Think about how what you are reading is related to other information that you know.

For example, as you read the public transport report:
• You might remember hearing about an accident that happened when a concrete pillar collapsed at the bus station.
• You might remember talking to a friend about how there was no bus service to a new suburb.
• You might remember reading about the financial difficulties that the council has had recently.

If you can show how different ideas are linked, you will get better marks for your essay.

All the ideas in the example are related. Your essay might explain that:
• The bus routes are out of date.
• The bus station might need to be repaired because the council cannot afford to build a new one.

You should also think about whether the information in the text disagrees with other texts that you have read.

For example, a different text might explain that the new suburb is close to a railway line. Therefore, you might decide that a train service would be better than re-organising the bus routes.

ACTIVITY 15.3

Think critically about a text.

1   Look at the text that you read in Activity 15.2.
2   How is it related to other information that you know?
3   How does it disagree with other information that you know?
4   How will these different ideas affect what you write in your essay?
5   Explain your ideas to a friend.

Time suggested:
10–15 minutes

A dictionary is not always useful when you are reading for research.

Why is a dictionary sometimes not useful?

Using a dictionary when you are reading for research can make your reading slow and less efficient. If you stop to check every word that you do not know, you will take much longer to read a text. When you are reading for research, you need to read quickly so that you can spend more time writing. In addition, if you look up a lot of words it is more difficult to remember the meaning of the whole text.

If you use a dictionary a lot, you may not develop good 'word attack' skills. This means that you might rely on the dictionary instead of trying to understand the meaning of a word.

In addition, a dictionary does not help you to remember new words. This is because it gives you a quick answer, instead of encouraging you to enlarge your vocabulary.

If you use a bi-lingual dictionary, like a Chinese-English or Spanish-English, you will teach yourself to translate. If you want to write well in English, you should try to think in English. Most people who study English do not want to become interpreters. Also some bi-lingual dictionaries are not up to date; some have inaccurate translations.

Checkpoint

How much do you rely on a dictionary to check new words?

Does your dictionary use help your reading, or does it make your reading slower than it needs to be?

_____

_____

How can you learn to manage without a dictionary?

When you read a new word, check whether the writer has explained it in the text. Many writers give a definition of technical words, especially the first time they use them.

If there is no explanation, try to understand new words by looking at the rest of the text. You may not need to know the exact meaning of the unfamiliar word. Of course, if the word is very important for that text, you might need to check it. However, you will often find that you can understand without using the dictionary.

Spend time learning and practising new vocabulary. When you learn a new word, find the meanings of words in the same word 'family'. For instance, if you learn "ability", you should also find and learn the meanings of "disability", "disabled", "disable", "inability", "unable" and "enable".

Learn words that will be useful for you. Check whether a word is used often. You can do this by looking at the frequency symbols in a learners dictionary. Learn the technical words that you need for your study, even if they are not usually used in everyday English. Do not spend time and effort learning words that you will not need.

If you do use a dictionary, use an English-English one. While it is quick and easy to use a bilingual dictionary, you do not always need to know the translation of a word. Many words cannot be translated precisely, anyway. Make sure that your dictionary is a suitable one. You should be able to understand it easily, and it should contain the words that you need to know. Look at the box on page 162 for advice about choosing a dictionary that is suitable for you.

Reading without a dictionary

- Check whether the writer has explained a technical word.
- Try to understand new vocabulary by looking at the rest of the text.
- Spend time learning and practising new vocabulary.
- Learn word families.
- Learn useful words.
- Do not try to translate.

Train your mind

1 Read as much as possible.
2 Practise scanning and skimming.
3 Practise reading texts fast and more than once.
4 Use the surrounding information to work out the meanings of new words.
5 Use a dictionary only if it is really important.

Choosing a suitable dictionary

1 Choose a dictionary that **you can understand**. Look at the explanations for several words. If you can understand them, then the dictionary is right for you. If you can not understand the explanations, find another dictionary.

2 Choose a dictionary that **includes sentences to show how to use each word**. There is not much point in learning what a word means if you do not know how to use it.

3 Choose a dictionary that is **up to date**. New words are being developed all the time. If a dictionary is more than about five years old, it will not contain modern words like "SARS", "modem", or "internet". If even these simple words are missing, there will be many more advanced words that will also be omitted.

4 Choose a dictionary that is **accurate**. Some electronic dictionaries do not include all the meanings for specific words. Some include meanings that are no longer used. Some have incorrect translations.

5 Choose a dictionary that **explains similar words in different ways**. For example, if a dictionary explains that "convince" means "to persuade", and "persuade" means "to convince", you will not learn anything.

6 Choose a dictionary that is **the right size**. If you use a paper dictionary, it should be small enough to carry around, but big enough to contain a useful number of words. Very small dictionaries often have too few words to be useful for advanced learners. You may want to buy two dictionaries: one for home use and one for your bag. If you always carry a dictionary with you, you are more likely to use it.

7 Choose an **English-English dictionary**, even if English is not your first language. If you use a bilingual dictionary (e.g. Spanish-English), you will teach yourself to be a translator. However, if you are writing in English then you really want to think in English. If you can read and understand this book, you are an advanced student of English; you have passed the stage of needing to translate.

8 Choose **more than one dictionary** if necessary. If you are studying a specialist discipline, it is a good idea to buy a specialist dictionary. For example, if you are studying microbiology, you probably need a dictionary with special scientific vocabulary, as well as a general dictionary.

Summarise the chapter

Research reading	Purpose
Reasons for special reading strategies	• • •
Strategies	Research questions and keywords • • •
	Scan • • •
	Skim •
	Reading more carefully • • •
	Thinking critically • • •

Using a dictionary	Not always useful
	•
	•
	•
	•
	Managing without
	•
	•
	•
	•
	•

► Check your understanding

Choose the correct answers.
Check whether they are correct (page 287).
If they are not correct, read the information in this chapter again.

1 When you are reading a text for research, you should read every word carefully. True or false?

2 You need to use special strategies for research reading because:
   a you want to work quickly and find information that is correct and relevant
   b your teacher wants you to hurry up and find as much information as possible
   c your teacher wants you to record all the references
   d all of the above.

3 When you scan, you should read as much information as possible. True or false?

4 When you skim read, you should:
   a find where the writer has placed the thesis statement and look for response questions
   b find all the unfamiliar words and look for explanations
   c find where the writer has placed the topic sentences and look for key words.

5 Scanning and skimming are not enough if you are looking for details about a subject. True or false?

6 If you read a text several times, you will usually:
   a get bored and want to stop
   b understand all the new words
   c understand the general meaning better.

7 When you read for research, you should think about how the information links with what you already know. True or false?

8 When you think critically about a text, you should:
   a think about how it agrees and disagrees with other texts
   b think about how it agrees with other texts
   c think about how it disagrees with other texts.

9 If you use a dictionary to check every new word, you will develop good word 'attack' skills. True or false?

10 When you learn a new word, you should:
   a write down the meaning in your notes
   b learn other words in the same word family
   c check it in a bi-lingual dictionary.

16 Making notes and paraphrasing

Learning outcomes

When you have finished studying this chapter, you should be able to:

1 identify relevant information and ideas for your essay;

2 make notes, using your own words.

Making notes for writing is different from other note making.

What are the differences?

When you are writing for study, you often need to record most of the information that you read. You need to do this because you will need all the information later when you are revising for examinations. You must take special notice of important information that is new for you. In addition, you might spend quite a lot of time making notes, because you are learning at the same time.

When you make notes as part of your essay research, you should record only the information and ideas that will be useful for your essay. You may need to record information and ideas that you already know, as well as what is new. You want to spend as much time as possible writing. Therefore, you must work as quickly as possible on note making while still doing a good job.

Are there any similarities?

Whatever your reason for making notes, you must spend time thinking. This is very important.

When you are doing general study, you must think so that you can learn. It is not possible to learn unless you understand what you are reading and recording. There is more information about thinking and learning in Chapter 11, pages 108–110.

When you are making notes for writing, you must think carefully so that you can organise the essay effectively. In particular, you must think about:

- the meaning of the information that you have read
- which ideas or pieces of information are useful for your essay
- where you should place them in your essay.

You should be selective about the information that you record.

What information should you choose?

You should choose only the information and ideas that help to answer your research questions and response questions.

Suppose that you were writing an argumentative essay about global warming.
- The thesis statement might be: We must act quickly to prevent further global warming.
- Some of the response questions might be:
    - What is global warming?
    - What effect has it already had?
    - What effect will it have if it continues?

You should make notes only about information that helps to

Of course, you should sometimes be flexible. You may find some information or an idea that you did not think of when you were planning. Then you might add a new response question to your outline, or a new topic sentence.

You might find a text that suggests that global warming might have some benefits. This is an interesting idea, and it is relevant to your essay. Therefore, you could add another response question to your essay outline: What positive effects might global warming have?

If that happens, you should make a note of the information that you find.

You must avoid plagiarising.

What can you do to avoid plagiarising?

You should **record all the references** while you are making notes.

If you do this, your list of references will be accurate, and you will save time later.

For instance, the information used in the examples in this chapter came from the *Wikipedia* website. The APA reference is: Global warming. (2005). *Wikipedia*. Retrieved March 28, 2005 from the Wikipedia website: http://en.wikipedia.org/wiki/Global_warming

As well as avoiding plagiarism, you will be able to find the sources of information again, if you need to.

paraphrase use your own words to explain the meaning of what someone else has written or said

It is easier to avoid plagiarising if you **paraphrase when you make your notes**.

This means that you must explain the information in your own words. This sounds simple. However, it is actually quite difficult to do, especially if English is not your first language. The vocabulary that you read is often complicated and difficult to explain.

Some of the information that you find about global warming might use specialist vocabulary, like "ecosystems", "evaporation" and "emissions".

Sometimes, you may be tempted to copy the words in a text. You might not understand the explanations very well. You might think that you cannot explain them in your own words.

For example, the following sentence is quite complicated and difficult to understand.

"Due to potential effects on human health and economy due to impact on the environment, global warming is a cause of great concern." (Global warming, 2005)

Sometimes, the explanations might sound much clearer than you can write.

The last part of the example above is very clear and simple. So is the next sentence: "Some important environmental changes have been observed and linked to global warming." (Global warming, 2005)

If you copy someone else's words in your notes, it will be difficult to use your own words when you write your essay. As a result, you will be more likely to plagiarise, and you will lose marks.

You can **use the TIRC formula to help you paraphrase**. You must follow four steps:

TIRC formula Think, Imagine, Record, Compare; used for paraphrasing

1	Think
2	Imagine
3	Record
4	Compare

You can use a mnemonic to help you remember the steps. You could use **T**hinking **I**s **R**eally **C**rafty, or you could think of your own mnemonic.

Checkpoint

If you want to, think of your own mnemonic to help you remember the four steps in the TIRC formula.

Step 1 Think

Think carefully about the meaning of what you have read or heard. Thinking takes time. However, it is worthwhile because it will help you to understand the subject more clearly. If you understand what you read, it is easier to use your own words. You should *never* write anything that you do not understand.

> Look again at the sentences from the example about global warming:
>
> "Due to potential effects on human health and economy due to impact on the environment, global warming is a cause of great concern. Some important environmental changes have been observed and linked to global warming." (Global warming, 2005)

Checkpoint

Think carefully about the meaning of the example above. (Do not use a dictionary unless you really cannot understand it.)

Step 2 Imagine

Imagine that you are explaining the idea to someone. Choose a friend or relative who does not know anything about the subject. Think about what you would tell that person.
- If you are alone, say the actual words aloud.
- If you do not want to disturb other people, 'say' the actual words in your head.

Many people find that thinking of a younger person helps them to make the explanation clear and simple.

> If you were explaining to a friend, you might change the order of the ideas. For example, you might begin by saying that global warming is a serious problem. Then you might say something about how it affects people's lives.

Checkpoint

Imagine that you are explaining this idea to a friend. Say your explanation aloud if possible, or 'say' it in your head.

Step 3 Record

Record what you said in Step 2. Write the exact words that you used. Read them carefully to make sure that your explanation is clear.

Checkpoint

Write the exact words that you said when you were imagining an explanation. _____

_____

_____

You might write something like: Global warming is serious because it is already affecting the environment. This may be dangerous for people's well-being.

Step 4 Compare

Compare the words that you have written with the original. Make sure that you have not accidentally used the same set of words. You can repeat one or two words, especially if they are simple. However, you should not use them in the same order as they appear in the original.

The paraphrase above repeats "global warming" and "environment". These are very common words that people use often and understand easily. If you tried to replace them with different words, your explanation would be very long. If you copy more than one or two words, you should use quotation marks (" ...") in your notes. Add a reference so that you will remember that they are not your own words.

Checkpoint

Look at the words that you wrote in the last checkpoint.

Compare them with the original sentences, and with the example above.

Did you include all the important ideas?

Take care when you are paraphrasing

Some people get impatient when they are paraphrasing. Instead of using the TIRC formula, they replace each word in the original sentences with a word that means the same. They often use a dictionary to help them.

This method is really very similar to plagiarising. The result is often not clear. It may not make sense at all, especially if they have used a bilingual dictionary.

If you follow the four steps of the TIRC formula, you will avoid these problems.

ACTIVITY 16.1

Time suggested:
As long as you need

Use the TIRC formula to paraphrase information and ideas.

Use your own paper for this activity.

1 Find written information that will be useful for an essay that you are writing.

2 Use the TIRC formula to paraphrase it.
- **Think** carefully about the meaning.
- **Imagine** that you are explaining the information and ideas to a friend. Say the words aloud, or in your head.
- **Record** the exact words that you used. Check that your meaning is clear.
- **Compare** your writing with the original text.

3 When you have finished, discuss with a friend.

You can use several different note-making styles.

What styles can you use?

The way that you make notes will depend on your specific needs, and the way that you like to learn. It is a good idea to try different ways until you can work quickly and effectively.

You can begin to make notes while you are reading.

Some people find it helpful to photocopy useful texts, and write on them. This is a quick, easy and effective use of time.

For instance, you could photocopy a paper from a journal, or print it if you found it on an electronic database. Then you could use a highlighter or pen to mark useful points.

You can paste or photocopy information onto a large sheet of paper, and make notes on the margin

If you did this, it would look like the example in Figure 16.1 (page 172).

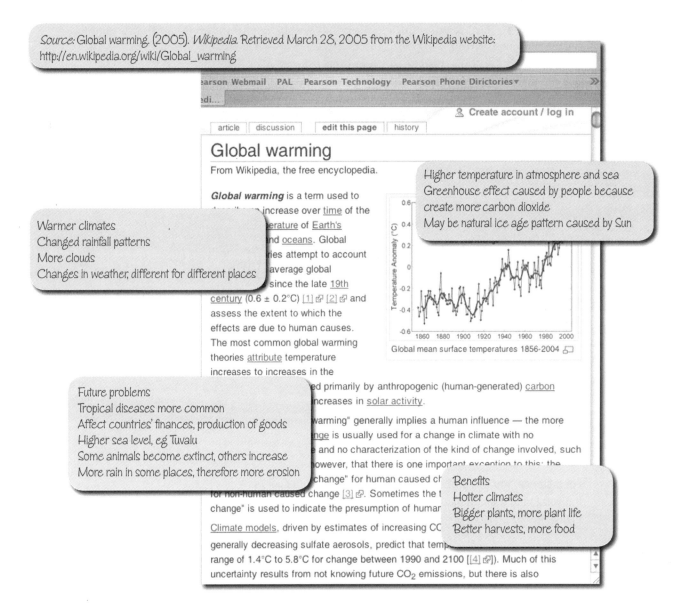

Figure 16.1   Notes about global warming recorded while reading

Source: Global warming. (2005) *Wikipedia*. Retrieved March 28, 2005 from the Wikipedia website:
http://en.wikipedia.org/wiki/Global_warming

You can **make notes directly onto your essay outline**.

This is especially useful if you are using a personal computer (PC) while you are researching. It is easy to cut and paste useful information.

If you did this, your outline would look like the one in Figure 16.2 (below).

If you are not using a computer, write each topic sentence on a separate piece of paper. As you read, add your notes to the correct topic sentence. It is a good idea to make a brief note about the source, next to each note.

Thesis statement:	We must act quickly to prevent global warming.
Response questions:	What is global warming?
	What effect has it already had?
	What effect will it have if it continues?
	What positive effects might it have?
Topic sentences:	Global warming is a condition where the world's atmosphere and oceans have become warmer.
	Greenhouse effect caused by people because they create more carbon dioxide
	May be natural ice age pattern caused by the Sun
	There are signs that global warming has already begun.
	Changed rainfall patterns
	More clouds
	Changes in weather, different for different places
	There will be serious consequences if global warming continues.
	Tropical diseases more common
	Affect countries' finances and production of goods
	Higher sea levels, e.g. Tuvalu
	Some animals may become extinct, others may increase in number
	More rain in some places, therefore more erosion
	On the other hand, global warming may have some positive effects.
	Warmer climates
	Bigger plants, more plant life
	Possibly better harvests, more food
	However, the disadvantages are likely to outweigh the benefits.
	Widespread effects, rapid change.

Figure 16.2 Notes about global warming, recorded as an essay outline

Source: Global warming. (2005) *Wikipedia*. Retrieved March 28, 2005 from the Wikipedia website: http://en.wikipedia.org/wiki/Global_warming

You can **make a mind map** with clusters of information.

Write the thesis statement in the middle of a large piece of paper. Write the response questions around the centre, with the clusters of the relevant topic sentences next to them. Then add your notes alongside each topic sentence.

The mind map might look like Figure 16.3 (below).

If you use this method, your notes must be very brief. You may need to use another method to record the details.

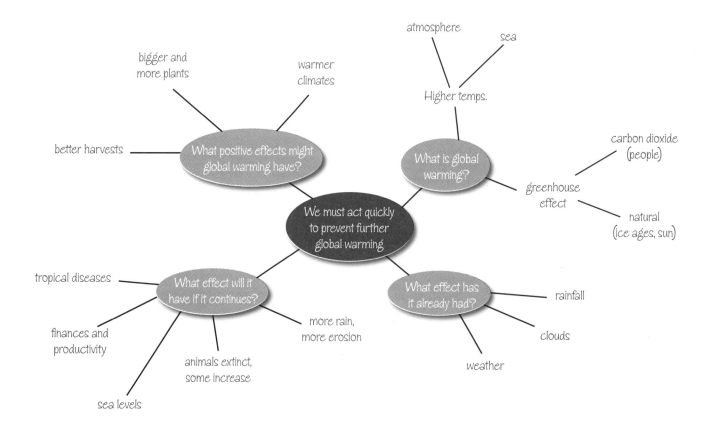

Figure 16.3 Notes about global warming, recorded as a mind map

Source: Global warming. (2005). *Wikipedia*. Retrieved March 28, 2005 from the Wikipedia website: http://en.wikipedia.org/wiki/Global_warming

You can **use a table** to organise the information.

This is another method that you can use if you are working on a computer. Make a table with two columns. Write the topic sentences in separate rows in the left column. Write each note in the right column, next to the appropriate topic sentence.

If you did this, your notes would look like Figure 16.4 (below).

When you have finished making notes, it is easy to re-arrange the information into order. The information in each row becomes part of a separate paragraph.

Global warming	
Global warming is a condition where the world's atmosphere and oceans have become warmer.	· Greenhouse effect caused by people because create more carbon dioxide · Maybe natural ice age pattern caused by the Sun
There are signs that global warming has already begun.	· Changed rainfall patterns · More clouds · Changes in weather, different for different places
There will be serious consequences if global warming continues.	· Tropical diseases more common · Affect countries' finances and production of goods · Higher sea level, e.g. Tuvalu · Some animals become extinct, others increase in number · More rain in some places, therefore more erosion
On the other hand, global warming may bring some positive results.	· Warmer climates · Bigger plants, more plant life · May be better harvests, more food
However, the overall result will have more disadvantages than benefits.	· Widespread effects, rapid change

Figure 16.4 Notes about global warming, recorded as a table

Source: Global warming. (2005). Wikipedia. Retrieved March 28, 2005 from the Wikipedia website: http://en.wikipedia.org/wiki/Global_warming

ACTIVITY 16.2

Time suggested:
As long as you need

Make notes for an essay.

Use your own paper for this activity.

1 Find written information that will be useful for an essay that you are writing. You can use the same essay as for Activity 16.1, or you can choose a different one.

2 Choose a note-making style and use it to make notes.
   - Use your own words.
   - Use the TIRC formula to help you.
   - Record each reference.

3 When you have finished, discuss your notes with a friend.

Train your mind

1 Practise using different vocabulary to explain the same information.

2 Practise using the TIRC formula.

3 Try different note-making styles until you find which one suits you.

Summarise the chapter

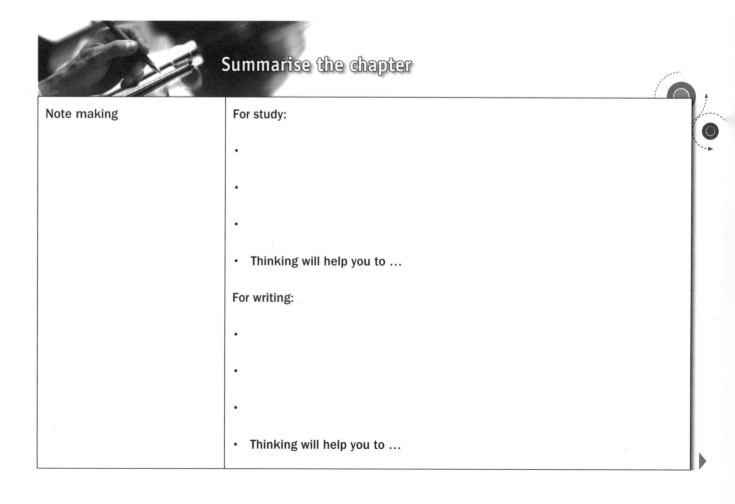

Note making	For study:
	•
	•
	•
	• Thinking will help you to …
	For writing:
	•
	•
	•
	• Thinking will help you to …

Selecting information	•
	•
Avoiding plagiarism	•
	•
Paraphrasing	Use TIRC formula
	T
	I
	R
	C
Note-making styles	Make notes while you are reading
	•
	Make notes directly onto essay outline
	•
	Make a mind map
	•
	•
	•
	Use a table
	•
	•

Check your understanding

Choose the correct answers.

Check whether they are correct (page 287).

If they are not correct, read the information in this chapter again.

1 When you are note making for writing, you should:

   a record all the information that you read

   b record information that you already know as well as what is new

   c record only information that is new.

2 The different sorts of note making have no similarities. True or false?

3 When you are making notes, you can sometimes add a response question to the essay outline. True or false?

4 If you record the reference details while you are note making:

   a it will be easier to avoid plagiarism

   b you will save time later

   c you will be able to find the sources again if necessary

   d all of the above.

5 When you paraphrase, you must place quotation marks around the exact words that someone else has written. True or false?

6 The TIRC formula is:

   a **T**hesis statement, **I**magination, **R**esponse questions, **C**ompare

   b **T**hink, **I**magine, **R**espond, **C**hange

   c **T**hink, **I**magine, **R**ecord, **C**ompare.

7 If you use your own words when you make notes, you will find it easier to use your own words when you write the essay. True or false?

8 Thinking takes time, but it is very important. True or false?

9 When you paraphrase a text, you can use the same sentence structure, but you must change most of the words. True or false?

10 It is a good idea to practise using different note-making styles because:

   a you want to find the style that suits you best

   b you will get bored if you always use the same style

   c you can explain them to your friends if you know them all.

SECTION

6

Writing

This section discusses how to write the first draft of an essay. It gives suggestions about writing clearly and about organising the essay in a logical way. It also includes information about using citations and transition signals. Finally, it gives guidelines for writing introductory and concluding paragraphs.

17 Writing the first draft

When you have finished studying this chapter, you should be able to:

1 explain how to use your planning and research materials to write a first draft;

2 explain how to make your explanations clear and concise;

3 explain how to make your writing persuasive.

The first draft is when the writing begins to look like an essay.

What does the first draft contain?

first draft the stage of the writing process when you use sentences to develop the outline

At the first draft stage, you work on the content of your essay. You think about the ideas that you developed and the information that you gathered when you were planning and researching. Then you put them together. This may be the first time in your essay preparation that you write in full sentences.

How should you organise the writing process?

You should begin by deciding which information and ideas belong together.

1 Look at the essay outline. If you were writing an essay about Sydney as a holiday destination, your outline might look like this:

Outline for essay about Sydney as a holiday destination

Thesis statement:	Sydney is a good place to go for a holiday.
Response questions:	Why is Sydney a good holiday destination?
	What attractions does Sydney offer tourists?
Topic sentences:	Visitors to Sydney can enjoy water sports.
	Sydney has a multicultural society.
	The mountains nearby offer a variety of outdoor activities.
	Sydney enjoys a pleasant climate.
	There is plenty to do and see in the city.
	Sydney is also suitable for a relaxing holiday.

2   Look at the information that you have collected. You should look at all your
notes: the information from your research and any mind maps or diagrams
that you have made. For instance, you might have information about:
*   the average temperatures in summer and winter
*   information about rainfall
*   the places that are especially popular for water ski-ing and sailing
*   the areas with beaches that are suitable for surfing
*   the areas with beaches that are safe for swimming
*   cultural attractions
*   the areas where people can explore caves and go rock climbing
*   the national parks that are especially popular for bushwalking
*   the main attractions in Sydney city
*   information about diving
*   the nature reserves with beautiful scenery.

Checkpoint

Think about which pieces of information (above) belong with each topic sentence in the outline
(page 180).

3   Decide which pieces of information belong to each topic sentence. If you are
writing by hand, it is a good idea to write each topic sentence on a separate
piece of paper. Then it is easy to record each piece of information in the right
place. If you are using a computer, you can use a table. Your table would
look like this, although it would have more detail:

Topic sentences	Information and ideas
Visitors to Sydney can enjoy water sports.	The areas with beaches that are suitable for surfing The areas with beaches that are safe for swimming Diving The places that are especially popular for water ski-ing and sailing
Sydney has a multicultural society.	Cultural attractions
The mountains nearby offer a variety of outdoor activities.	The areas where people can explore caves and go rock climbing The national parks that are especially popular for bushwalking
Sydney enjoys a pleasant climate.	The average temperatures in the summer and winter Rainfall
There is also plenty to do and see in the city.	The main attractions in Sydney city
Sydney is also suitable for a relaxing holiday.	The nature reserves with beautiful scenery Beaches

ACTIVITY 17.1

Time suggested:
As long as you need

Match research information with topic sentences.

Use your own paper for this activity.

1 Look at the outline for an essay that you are writing.

2 Look at the information and ideas that you have collected.

3 Decide which pieces of information belong with each topic sentence.
   • Use a table if you are working on the computer.
   • Use pieces of paper if you are writing by hand.

Once you have clustered the information in this way, you can write a paragraph about each topic sentence. It is important to make sure that your explanations are clear and easy to understand.

Your explanations must be clear and concise.

What does "concise" mean?

concise avoiding unnecessary words so that explanations are short and concentrate on the subject

When you write concisely, you avoid unnecessary words. Your explanations are short and concentrate on the subject that you are writing about.

How can you make sure that your writing is clear and concise?

You can 'speak inside your head'. This method is often used by writers who have auditory learning preferences. It is especially useful if you have difficulty explaining exactly what you want to say. Sometimes, you can organise your thoughts by imagining how you would explain them in a simple way:

• to a younger person

• to a friend who does not know about the subject.

Of course, you can speak aloud if you are alone. Some writers like to use a dictaphone or tape recorder to help them explain clearly.

KISS principle
Keep It Short and Simple

You can use the KISS principle to make your explanations clear. KISS is a mnemonic that stands for Keep It Short and Simple. If you use short words and sentences, your writing will be easier to understand.

• **Use short words that are suitable for your reader.**

If you use words that are too difficult, your reader will not be able to understand what you have written.

In the essay about Sydney, many people would find it difficult to understand your meaning if you wrote: The mountainous ranges of this area of terra firma offer a multitude of recreational activities that are eminently suitable for undertaking in an alfresco environment.

You should choose vocabulary that your reader will understand.

Your explanation would be much clearer if you wrote something like:
The mountains nearby offer a variety of outdoor activities.

However, if you use very simple words, adult or knowledgeable readers may lose interest and stop reading.

This example would be suitable for small children, but not for adults:
There are some mountains near Sydney. You can do a lot of things there.

Checkpoint

What sort of vocabulary is suitable for the target reader of *your* essays? _____

_____

_____

- **Use short sentences.**

Most readers find it difficult to understand sentences that are longer than about 20 words.

Look again at the sentence that begins, "The mountainous ranges of this area of terra firma … "(example, page 182). As well as having difficult vocabulary, it is also too long. There are too many words for the reader to understand at one time.

However, too many very short sentences will make your writing sound jerky and unconnected. It is a good idea to use different lengths of sentence. Some can be very short, others longer.

Checkpoint

What sort of sentences do *you* write?

Are they usually short and easy to understand?

Are they often long and difficult?

Do you use a mixture of lengths? _____

_____

_____

- Use words carefully.

Do not use unnecessary words.

For example, consider this sentence: At present, the number of tourists is much higher now than it was in the 1980s.

"At present" and "now" have the same meaning. You should use only one of them.

Do not use meaningless phrases.

For instance:
- "In this world of ours" has no meaning because you are unlikely to be writing about life on another planet.
- "In three short years" is also meaningless because every year has the same length.

Do not repeat ideas.

If you are writing about relaxing by the sea, you do not need to repeat information about swimming at the beach. Therefore, you should avoid phrases like, "As I have already said ...".

Checkpoint

Do *you* write concisely?

Think about any problems that you have. _____

_____

_____

ACTIVITY 17.2

Time suggested:
As long as you need

Write a first draft.

Use your own paper for this activity.

1   Write a first draft of the essay that you began in Activity 17.1.
- Use the information that you collected and the outline that you developed.
- Write in sentences.
- Use the KISS principle to make sure that your explanations are clear and concise.

2   When you have finished, discuss what you did, with a friend.

As well as using the KISS principle, **you should use vocabulary correctly**. If you use a word incorrectly, the reader will not understand what you mean. For example, if you write "hyperglycaemia" instead of "hypoglycaemia", the sentence will mean the opposite of what you want to say. If you use "poignant" instead of "to the point" the reader will not be able to understand you at all.

You should also **use words that sound interesting**. You want your reader to keep reading. Therefore, you should avoid clichés (pronounced "clee-shays"). These are common sayings that have been used so much that they sound boring. Some examples of clichés are:

> **cliché** a common saying that has been used so much that it sounds boring

- better late than never
- blood is thicker than water
- as white as a sheet
- in this day and age
- there is no garden without weeds.

Checkpoint

Think of some other clichés that you should avoid. _____

_____

_____

_____

You must use your own words. If you plagiarise (copy someone else's words), you are more likely to use information that is not relevant or useful. You are also more likely to use vocabulary that you do not understand, and it may be incorrect. You should *never* write anything that you do not understand. You will also lose marks if you plagiarise, so it is not worthwhile.

ACTIVITY 17.3

Time suggested: 10 minutes

Check your vocabulary.

1 Check the words that you used in the first draft of your essay (from Activity 17.2).

Check that you have used:
- correct vocabulary
- interesting words
- your own words.

2 Discuss what you did, with a friend.

When you write an argumentative essay, you should make your writing persuasive.

Why should you write persuasively in an argumentative essay?

The purpose of an argumentative essay is quite different from that of an expository essay. When you are arguing about something, you want to persuade your reader to accept your point of view. Therefore, you must choose your words carefully.

What words can you use to make your writing persuasive?

You can **use words that express your ideas in a 'strong' way**.

This is different from an expository essay.

Suppose that you were writing about the importance of preventing child abuse. If your essay was expository, you could write something like:
- Child abuse can cause psychological problems in adulthood.
or
- Children who are abused may grow into abusive adults.

In an argumentative essay, it would be more effective to express your ideas more forcefully.

In an argumentative essay, you could write:
- Abused children grow into adults with psychological problems, and our society suffers as a result. This must not be allowed to continue.

You can **use words that appeal to the reader's emotions or better feelings**.

If you do this, you can suggest that your opinion is right from a moral point of view.

For example, you could write:
- No right-minded person could justify the sort of child abuse that leads to mental illness.

Remember that you must justify your opinions. Your reader will not accept your persuasive writing if you do not support it with information. If you use information from other people's writing, you must use citations. (See Chapter 19, pages 201–212.)

You can also **make your language stronger by avoiding the word "I"**. Some people use phrases like "I think …" or "In my opinion …" in their essays. This tells the reader that the statement is the writer's point of view, and suggests that the reader might not agree. A statement without "I" sounds more like a fact, even if it is an opinion. Therefore the reader is more likely to accept it, especially if it is followed by a clear explanation. Look at these examples:

I think that Hawaiian pizza is delicious.	Hawaiian pizza is delicious.
I believe that all parents should have child-rearing training.	All parents should have child-rearing training.
I would like to suggest that the government must do more to eradicate poverty.	The government must do more to eradicate poverty.
In my opinion, children who eat a lot of junk food will grow into obese adults.	Children who eat a lot of junk food will grow into obese adults.

Checkpoint

Which column contains the strongest language? Why? _____

_____

_____

ACTIVITY 17.4

Time suggested: 20–30 minutes

Practise using strong persuasive language.

Use your own paper for this activity.

1 Choose five of the thesis statements in the list below.
2 For each one, think of:
   • a sentence that would be suitable for an expository essay
   • a stronger sentence that would be suitable for an argumentative essay.
3 Write the sentences in a table, with one column for expository writing and one for argumentative writing.
4 Explain to a friend why your expository and argumentative sentences are different.

Thesis statements

a It is cruel to keep animals in zoos.
b The public transport system needs to be improved.
c Smoking is bad for your health.
d Sydney is a good tourist destination.
e Teenagers are dangerous drivers.
f Learning a second language is a useful skill.
g Conservation is everyone's responsibility.
h Tourism is ruining the environment.
i Mobile phones can damage children's health.
j Computer skills are important.

ACTIVITY 17.5   **Write persuasively in a short argumentative essay.**

Time suggested:
As long as you need

Use your own paper for this activity.

1   Choose an issue to write about. You can use:
    • one of the thesis statements in the list below
    • one of the thesis statements in Activity 17.4
    • one of the outlines that you developed in Chapter 10
    • a different issue that you feel strongly about.

2   Develop an essay outline, if you do not already have one.

3   Check the outline to make sure that it uses TRT and a classical structure. (See Chapters 8 and 10 if you need information.)

4   Write the first draft of a short argumentative essay. Remember to write persuasively.

5   Discuss what you did, with a friend.

Thesis statements for an argumentative essay

a   Everyone should learn a second language.
    or
    There is no need for people to speak more than one language.

b   Conservation is an individual responsibility.
    or
    Conservation is the government's responsibility.

c   The drinking age should be raised.
    or
    The drinking age should not be raised.

d   The government must pay students' tertiary fees.
    or
    Tertiary students must pay their own study fees.

e   People with smoking-related illnesses should pay for their own medical treatment.
    or
    The government should provide free medical treatment for everyone.

Train your mind

1   Write often, every day if possible.

2   Find five words every day and think of other words with the same meaning.

3   Practise "speaking in your head" to see if it helps you to explain clearly.

4   Listen for clichés and think about how to replace them.

5   Remember the persuasive words that people use when they are discussing issues.

Summarise the chapter

A first draft is ...	
Organising the writing process	Matching information and ideas • • •
Explaining clearly and concisely	'Speaking inside your head' • • KISS principle • K _ _ _ I _ S _ _ _ _ _ _ _ S _ _ _ _ _ • • Vocabulary use • • •
Writing persuasively	• • •

▶ Check your understanding

Choose the correct answers.
Check whether they are correct (page 287).
If they are not correct, read the information in this chapter again.

1 The first draft of an essay contains:
   a all the ideas that you thought of when you were brainstorming
   b the ideas that you have developed and the information that you have collected
   c all the information that you have collected when you were researching. ▶

2   When you write the first draft, you should use complete sentences. True or false?

3   When you *begin* to write the first draft, it is a good idea to:
   a   use your own words, avoiding clichés and complicated vocabulary
   b   match your words with the KISS principle
   c   match the topic sentences from your outline with the information from your research.

4   A concise explanation does not use unnecessary words. True or false?

5   You should *always* 'speak inside your head' when you are trying to write clearly. True or false?

6   If you use the KISS principle, your writing will be too simple for your target reader. True or false?

7   You should use short sentences because:
   a   your reader will understand them more easily
   b   your reader will find it easy to check the meaning of every word
   c   they will make the paragraphs more impressive.

8   You should take care with the vocabulary that you use because:
   a   if you use a word incorrectly, your meaning will not be clear
   b   "poignant" means the same as "to the point"
   c   long words will show your teacher that you know a lot.

9   If you avoid clichés, your essay will sound boring. True or false?

10 You can make your writing persuasive by:
   a   using 'strong' words
   b   suggesting that your opinion is morally right
   c   avoiding using "I"
   d   all of the above.

18 Organising paragraphs

Learning outcomes

When you have finished studying this chapter, you should be able to:

1 explain why paragraphs are useful;

2 explain how to plan and write paragraphs.

Paragraphs are useful tools for organising an essay.

What is a paragraph?

paragraph a group of sentences about one idea

A paragraph is a group of sentences that are placed together in an essay. Each paragraph explains or gives information about a different idea. Your essay outline is very useful at this stage because each topic sentence will summarise a separate paragraph.

Why are paragraphs useful?

There are two main reasons for using paragraphs.

- Paragraphs help the reader to understand the information in an essay. Reading an essay is a bit like eating a salami. Cutting a salami into slices or small pieces makes it easier to eat and digest. In the same way, organising the information in your essay into paragraphs will make it easier to read and understand.

- Writing that is split into paragraphs looks more inviting. If the reader thinks the writing looks attractive, s/he will want to read it. Compare the two examples on page 192. The information in both is the same but one looks better.

Example 1

"Structure" describes the way that something is organised. When you are writing an essay, you want the reader to understand your explanation and ideas. Therefore, you must organise the essay so that the reader can understand it easily. Every essay should have an introduction, a body and a conclusion. The introduction, at the beginning of the essay, tells the reader what the essay is about. The body contains the information and ideas that the writer wants the reader to understand. The conclusion is placed at the end of the essay. It shows the reader how the content in the body supports the main message of the essay. People use this structure for a lot of their communication with each other. For example, most telephone and face-to-face conversations, and most letters, have a beginning, a middle and an end. If one part is missing, the structure will be incomplete. Then the reader or listener will find it difficult to understand what the writer or speaker wants to say. An expository essay usually follows a simple structure. The writer organises the information so that the reader can understand it easily. The introduction usually contains some general information, as well as the subject and the writer's point of view (thesis statement). The body contains information that explains the thesis. You should arrange the information in the body in a logical order, so that the reader can understand it easily. You must take extra care with a comparative essay, because the information is more complicated.

Example 2

"Structure" describes the way that something is organised. When you are writing an essay, you want the reader to understand your explanation and ideas. Therefore, you must organise the essay so that the reader can understand it easily.

Every essay should have an introduction, a body and a conclusion. The introduction, at the beginning of the essay, tells the reader what the essay is about. The body contains the information and ideas that the writer wants the reader to understand. The conclusion is placed at the end of the essay. It shows the reader how the content in the body supports the main message of the essay.

People use this structure for a lot of their communication with each other. For example, most telephone and face-to-face conversations, and most letters, have a beginning, a middle and an end. If one part is missing, the structure will be incomplete. Then the reader or listener will find it difficult to understand what the writer or speaker wants to say.

An expository essay usually follows a simple structure. The writer organises the information so that the reader can understand it easily. The introduction usually contains some general information, as well as the subject and the writer's point of view (thesis statement). The body contains information that explains the thesis. You should arrange the information in the body in a logical order, so that the reader can understand it easily.

You must take extra care with a comparative essay, because the information is more complicated.

 Checkpoint

Which example looks more inviting? Why? _____

_____

The paragraphs should show unity.

What is unity?

> **unity** when everything in one place belongs together

Unity means that everything in one place belongs together. This means that each paragraph must contain information about only one idea. For longer essays, or for complicated subjects, you may need more than one paragraph for each idea. However, it is always important that every paragraph can be read and understood easily.

How can you make sure that each paragraph has unity?

You can use the SEX formula to make sure that a paragraph has unity. SEX is a mnemonic that stands for:

> **SEX formula** a way of organising a paragraph; includes statement, explanation and extra details

> Statement
>
> Explanation
>
> eXtra details

- **The statement** is the topic sentence that helps to answer the response question(s). It summarises the whole paragraph and tells the reader what the paragraph is about. You should place it where the reader can easily notice it: at the beginning or end of the paragraph. If you 'bury' it in the middle, it will be more difficult to find. In Australia and New Zealand, topic sentences are often placed at the beginnings of paragraphs.
- **The explanation** usually follows the statement. It might contain a definition or a description, or it might give a reason for the information in the statement.
- **The extra details** add more information to the explanation so that the information is complete. Sometimes you can include an example that helps to make the meaning clearer.

The paragraph below shows how the SEX formula can be used for simple information.

S New Zealand enjoys a temperate climate. This means that there are no extremes of temperature. The summers are warm and the winters are mild. In the north,

E the average temperature is only 24° Celsius in summer, and 15° Celsius in winter. Even in the south of the South Island where it does sometimes snow, the average winter temperature is 9° Celsius. Any season is a good time for a holiday

X because it never gets very hot or very cold.

Notice the final sentence that has been added at the end of the paragraph. This sentence uses different words to repeat the idea in the topic sentence (statement). It also helps to link the paragraph with the thesis statement at the beginning of the essay.

Checkpoint

Look at other paragraphs in this book. Identify how they use the SEX formula.

ACTIVITY 18.1   **Use the SEX formula.**

1 Check the first draft that you wrote for the activities in Chapter 17, or use a different essay.
2 Make sure that you have used the SEX formula for every paragraph.
3 Discuss your paragraph structure with a friend.

Time suggested:
10 minutes

If you are writing about a complicated idea, you can use a SEXEX pattern. In this case, the statement, explanation and extra details are followed by some more explanation and further extra details. For example:

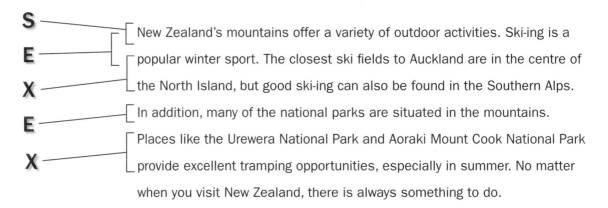

S — New Zealand's mountains offer a variety of outdoor activities. Ski-ing is a
E — popular winter sport. The closest ski fields to Auckland are in the centre of
X — the North Island, but good ski-ing can also be found in the Southern Alps.
E — In addition, many of the national parks are situated in the mountains.
X — Places like the Urewera National Park and Aoraki Mount Cook National Park provide excellent tramping opportunities, especially in summer. No matter when you visit New Zealand, there is always something to do.

In this example, the concluding paragraph does not repeat the topic sentence. Instead, it refers only to the thesis statement and reminds the reader what the essay is about.

Checkpoint

Find some paragraphs in this book that use the SEXEX pattern.

ACTIVITY 18.2

Time suggested: 10 minutes

Use the SEXEX formula.

1   Check the first draft that you used for Activity 18.1.
2   Make sure that you have used the SEXEX formula for any complicated paragraphs.
3   Discuss your paragraph structure with a friend.

If your teachers ask you to use references in your essays, you can use the **SEX-C** formula:

Statement

Explanation

eXtra details

Citation

Citations show the sources of the information that you have used in your essay. This means that they tell the reader where you found the information. A citation usually includes the author's name, or the title of the text if you do not know the name of the author. It includes the year of publication if this is available. Sometimes it also gives a page number. You should use citations whenever you use someone else's ideas in your essay. See Chapter 19 (pages 201–212) for information about using citations. The example below uses a citation to show where the writer found the information for the extra details in the paragraph.

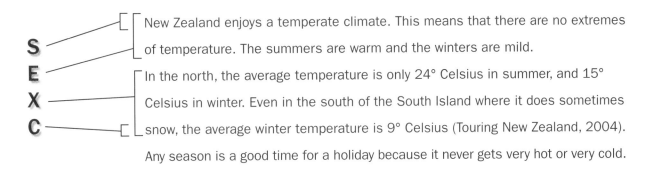

S New Zealand enjoys a temperate climate. This means that there are no extremes of temperature. The summers are warm and the winters are mild.

E
X In the north, the average temperature is only 24° Celsius in summer, and 15° Celsius in winter. Even in the south of the South Island where it does sometimes

C snow, the average winter temperature is 9° Celsius (Touring New Zealand, 2004).

Any season is a good time for a holiday because it never gets very hot or very cold.

You can adjust the SEX-C formula to fit the information that you are presenting. For instance:

- You must place a citation next to the information or ideas that you are quoting. Sometimes a citation will follow a statement. Sometimes it will follow an explanation or some extra details.
- Sometimes you may need to use more than one citation in a single paragraph. You might have found two sources about one piece of information. Alternatively, you might want to use citations for more than one part of the SEX formula.
- If the paragraph is complicated, you might need to use a SEX-C EX-C pattern.

Remember that you must also record information about every citation in the List of References. (See Chapter 14, pages 138–155.)

Checkpoint

Find some paragraphs in this book that use the SEX-C formula.

ACTIVITY 18.3   **Identify different sorts of paragraph.**

Time suggested:
10–15 minutes

Look at the sample essays on pages 275–282.
Find:
- a paragraph that uses SEX
- a paragraph that uses SEXEX
- a paragraph that uses SEX-C
- a paragraph that uses SEX-C EX-C.

The paragraphs should be coherent.

What is coherence?

coherent containing
information that is related

If your paragraphs are coherent, they will contain information that is related.

Although each paragraph is about a different idea,
all the paragraphs must link together to answer
the response question(s). As they do this, they will
also support the thesis statement.

In an essay about New Zealand as a holiday destination, each
paragraph could be about a different attraction in New Zealand.
However, all the paragraphs must be about why New Zealand is a good
choice for a holiday. You could not include information about another
country, or about industry in New Zealand.

coherent order organisation
of information so that
it is logical and easy to
understand

The paragraphs must also be organised into a coherent order. That is, they must be organised logically, so that the reader can understand the information more easily.

How can you make sure that the paragraphs are coherent?

When you are writing your essay, you should **use only information that is relevant**. You can check this by making sure that the topic sentences answer the response questions *in a direct way*. (See Chapter 8, pages 79–87, about the TRT formula.)

You should check that the **response question and each topic sentence fit together**.

You can do this by:
• asking a response question
• replying with the topic sentence.

For instance, suppose that you wanted to check the first topic sentence
in the essay about New Zealand. You could ask, "Why is New Zealand a
good holiday choice?" Then you could reply, "Because there are many
beautiful beaches." The answer fits well with the question, so you know
that this topic sentence is relevant.

If the question begins with "why", you can use "because" to help you answer it. You cannot do this for questions that begin with "what" or "where" or "when" or "how". However, you must still make sure that the topic sentence is a direct answer to the response question.

ACTIVITY 18.4

Begin to check that paragraphs are coherent.

1 Check the writing that you used for Activities 18.1–18.3.
2 Make sure that every topic sentence answers the response questions in a direct way.
3 Discuss your topic sentences with a friend.

Time suggested:
5–10 minutes

In addition, you should **organise the paragraphs into a coherent order**.
- You should arrange the paragraphs so that **similar ideas are placed together**.

This makes it easy for the reader to understand how they are related to each other.

Look at the outline (below) of an essay about New Zealand as a holiday destination. The topic sentences in this example outline are not arranged in any particular order. They need to be organised so that similar information is placed together.

Outline for essay about New Zealand as a holiday destination

Thesis statement:	New Zealand is a good place to go for a holiday.
Response questions:	Why is New Zealand a good holiday choice? What attractions does New Zealand offer tourists?
Topic sentences:	There are many beautiful beaches. New Zealand has a bi-cultural and multicultural society. New Zealand's mountains offer a variety of outdoor activities. Many of the lakes and rivers are suitable for water sports. The people are friendly. New Zealand enjoys a temperate climate, There is also plenty to do and see in the cities.

Checkpoint

Look at the topic sentences in the outline above.

Decide which paragraphs should be placed together.

- Sometimes the paragraphs are best arranged in **order of importance**. The paragraph with the most valuable or strongest idea is presented first. Then the next most valuable one is presented. This continues until all the ideas have been used, ending with the least important one.

order of importance
the most valuable idea is presented first, followed by the next most valuable idea, and so on

reverse order of importance
the weakest idea is presented first and the strongest idea last

chronological order
information is presented according to what happens first, second, third, etc.

- You could decide to organise the paragraphs in **reverse order of importance**. This is sometimes useful for argumentative essays. In this case, you would place the weakest idea first and the strongest idea last.
- Sometimes, you can organise the paragraphs into **chronological order**. This means that the information is presented in steps according to what happens first, second, third, etc. Chronological order is especially suitable for instructions or for stories where the timing is important.

Checkpoint

Think of two subjects where it would be a good idea to present information in chronological order.

ACTIVITY 18.5

Time suggested: 10 minutes

Organise paragraphs into chronological order.

The essay outline below is about building a garden wall. However, the topic sentences have not been organised into a coherent order.

Thesis statement:	Building a garden wall is not difficult if you work step by step.
Response questions:	What steps should I follow? What is the order of work?
Topic sentences:	As you build, check that each row of bricks is level. Shrubs and flowers planted nearby can make your wall look more attractive. Collect all the equipment together before you start to build. It is important to check the local council regulations. Take care with mixing the mortar. You are more likely to succeed if you make a plan. Make sure that the foundation is firm.

1 Organise the topic sentences into chronological order.
2 Discuss your answers with a friend. Give reasons for the order that you chose.

ACTIVITY 18.6

Time suggested: 10 minutes

Check paragraphs for coherent order.

1 Check the writing that you used for Activities 18.1–18.4.
2 Make sure that the paragraphs are arranged in a coherent order.
   - Are similar ideas placed near each other?
   - Have you used:
     – order of importance?
     – reverse order of importance?
     – chronological order?
3 Discuss your answers with a friend. Explain the reasons for the way you have organised the paragraphs.

Train your mind

1 Think about how different ideas belong together.
2 When you are reading, check whether or not the author has used the SEX or SEXEX formula.
3 When you are reading or writing, check whether or not the topic sentences answer the response questions in a direct way.
4 When you are reading or writing, check whether or not the paragraphs are arranged in a coherent order.

Summarise the chapter

A paragraph is ...	
Uses of paragraphs	• •
Unity happens when ...	
SEX formula	S E X
	SEXEX
SEX-C formula	C
Coherence	• Include relevant information • Check relevance • Arrange

Coherent order	•
	•
	•
	•

► Check your understanding

Choose the correct answers.

Check whether they are correct (page 287).

If they are not correct, read the information in this chapter again.

1 A paragraph is a group of ideas that are placed together. True or false?

2 Paragraphs are useful because:
   a they help make your writing easier to understand
   b they look more interesting and inviting than continuous writing
   c both the above.

3 If a paragraph shows unity, it contains:
   a information that agrees with the thesis statement
   b information that belongs together
   c clear explanations.

4 When we are talking about paragraphs, SEX stands for:
   a **S**ituation, **E**xplanation, e**X**tra details
   b **S**tatement, **E**xplanation, e**X**tra details
   c **S**tatement, **E**xtra details, e**X**planation.

5 You can use the SEXEX formula for
   a any sort of paragraph
   b very simple paragraphs
   c complicated paragraphs.

6 You can use the SEX-C formula when you are using citations in a paragraph. True or false?

7 If your paragraphs are coherent, they contain different ideas about the same subject. True or false?

8 If your paragraphs are coherent:
   a the topic sentences must answer the response questions in a direct way
   b the thesis statement must answer the response questions in a direct way
   c the response questions must be clear.

9 If you use reverse order of importance, the most important ideas should be placed at the beginning of the essay. True or false?

10 Chronological order means that:
   a the information is organised according to when something happens
   b the information is organised according to why something happened
   c the information is about building a garden wall.

19 Using quotations and citations

Learning outcomes

When you have finished studying this chapter, you should be able to:

1 explain what direct and indirect quotations are and when to use them;

2 explain how to use citations for direct and indirect quotations.

When you write, you can use indirect and direct quotations.

What is an indirect quotation?

indirect quotation a paraphrase of what someone has written or said; uses your own words

An **indirect quotation** is a paraphrase of what someone else has written or said.

> This means that you use your own words to explain the ideas or information that you found when you were researching a subject.

> > For instance, suppose that you are writing an essay about the effects of energy drinks on sports performance. You have found some general background information about how fitness levels affect sports performance. You can use your own words to explain what you have read.

> When you write an essay, your teacher is most interested in *your* ideas and *your* writing. Therefore, you should use your own words as much as possible.

> > Examples 1–6 on page 204 are indirect quotations.

**Time suggested:
10 minutes**

ACTIVITY 19.1

Identify indirect quotations.

1   Look at an essay that you are writing. You can use one that you wrote for the activities in Chapter 17, or you could choose a different one.
2   Find all the indirect quotations.
3   Mark them with a highlighter or pencil.
4   Check that you have used your own words.
5   Discuss your indirect quotations with a friend.

What is a direct quotation?

direct quotation the exact words that someone has written or said

A direct quotation contains the exact words that another person has written or said.

You usually use a direct quotation if an author has explained an important idea more clearly than you can.

The second point in your essay might be about how different substances affect sports performance. You have found some information about the effects of caffeine and guarana. This information is important because many energy drinks contain these chemicals. The explanation is very clear, so you decide to quote directly.

**Time suggested:
10 minutes**

ACTIVITY 19.2

Identify direct quotations.

1   Look at the essay that you used in Activity 19.1.
2   Find all the direct quotations.
3   Mark them with a highlighter or pencil. If possible, use a different colour from the one you used in Activity 19.1.
4   Check that you have copied the words correctly.
5   Discuss your direct quotations with a friend.

How should you use quotations?

An indirect quotation uses your own words. Therefore you must write it as an ordinary part of your essay text.

However, you must use a different format for direct quotations.

If a direct quotation is short, write it as part of your essay text and use double quotation marks.

If you are using APA format, "short" means fewer than 40 words. Universities that follow the Harvard system often suggest 30 words as a maximum for a short quotation.

Examples 7–10 on pages 204–205 are indirect quotations.

If the direct quotation is longer than 30 or 40 words, you do not need to use quotation marks. Instead, you should separate the quotation from your own writing, and use indentation to show that you are quoting.

Examples 11 and 12 on page 205 are long direct quotations.

You should use citations to support the quotations in your writing.

What is a citation?

A citation is a short record of a source of information that you have used in an essay. It tells the reader the details about where you found information. The source may be written or oral (spoken) or audio-visual.

Citations are used in addition to a list of references, but they are placed inside an essay. It is a good idea to record each reference as you write each citation so that nothing is left out by mistake. Chapter 14, pages 138–155, has detailed information about recording references.

citation a short record of a source of information that you have used in an essay; placed inside an essay

Why should you use citations?

There are four main reasons for using citations:

- Citations help to persuade your reader to accept your point of view. They do this by showing that you are not the only person who has your opinion. Your reader is more likely to believe you if s/he knows that other people agree with your ideas. S/he will be more convinced if your sources are people who are specialists in the subject that you are writing about.
- Citations tell the reader where to find more information about the subject. This is very useful if the reader is interested in the subject, or wants to check a detail.
- Citations help you to avoid plagiarising. You can use other people's ideas or words as long as you show where you found them.
- Citations also show your reader that you can research information and use it to support your ideas. This is very important if you are writing an essay as part of a study course.

When should you use citations?

You should use a citation whenever you refer to someone else's ideas in your essay. You must do this whether you use an indirect or a direct quotation.

Examples of citations

Indirect quotations (paraphrases)

1   Author's name and the date of publication both known; whole source cited in brackets

    Of course, people's general fitness levels affect their sports performance (McArdle, Katch & Katch, 2001).

2   Author's name unknown; whole source cited in brackets

    Many sports energy drinks contain electrolytes which affect the way that your body absorbs water (Sports energy drinks, 2001).

3   Date of publication unknown; whole source cited in brackets

    Even if an additive is not banned, there is sometimes an unspoken agreement that it should not be used. This is true of caffeine (The buzz on energy, n.d.).

4   More than one source; both sources cited in brackets

    Even if an additive is not banned, there is sometimes an unspoken agreement that it should not be used. This is true of caffeine (Spriet, 2002; The buzz on energy, n.d.).

5   Author's name and date of publication known; cited with only the date in brackets

    McArdle, Katch and Katch (2001) suggest that people's general fitness levels affect their sports performance.

    or

    According to McArdle, Katch and Katch (2001), people's general fitness levels affect their sports performance.

6   Oral source; whole source cited in brackets

    Many people do not realise that the drinks that they can buy in the supermarket or dairy may contain substances that are banned on the sports field (M.Keagan, personal communication, March 18, 2006).

Direct quotations

7   Part of a sentence; author's name, date of publication and page number known; some words not included; whole source cited in brackets

    Athletes should be aware that guarana, "promoted as an Amazonian wonder supplement, . . . is chemically identical to caffeine" (Richardson, 2002, p. A3).

8   Part of a sentence; author's name and page number unknown; date of publication known; whole source cited in brackets

    Many sports energy drinks contain electrolytes which "promote the absorption of water into your body during an endurance exercise" (Sports energy drinks, 2001, ¶ 12).

9   Separate sentence; author's name, date of publication and page number all unknown; whole source cited in brackets

Even if an additive is not banned, there is sometimes an unspoken agreement that it should not be used. "The use of caffeine to boost sports performance is considered to be cheating and against the ethics of sport" (The buzz on energy, n.d. para. 8).

10   Author's name included as part of sentence; some words not included; date of publication and page number cited in brackets.

Athletes should check ingredients carefully. For instance, Richardson (2002, p. A3) points out that guarana, which is "promoted as an Amazonian wonder supplement, . . . is chemically identical to caffeine".

or

Athletes should check ingredients carefully. According to Richardson, guarana, "promoted as an Amazonian wonder supplement, . . . is chemically identical to caffeine" (2002, p. A3).

11   More than 40 words; separate sentences; blocked and indented; author's name, date of publication and page number known; whole source cited in brackets.

Many additives can be dangerous for health.

> *An excess of caffeine could be risky for people with high blood pressure or cholesterol. Many of the drinks contain guarana, promoted as an Amazonian wonder supplement, but the main ingredient in guarana, guaranine, is chemically identical to caffeine. (Richardson, 2002, p. A3)*

Therefore it is important to check ingredients carefully.

12   More than 40 words; separate sentences; blocked and indented; author's name, date of publication and page number unknown; whole source cited in brackets.

Even if an additive is not banned, there is sometimes an unspoken agreement that it should not be used.

> *As with any drug, the use of caffeine to boost sports performance is considered to be cheating and against the ethics of sport. However, for most people, the greater concern is for the risks associated with its use before or during physical activity. (The buzz on energy, n.d. ¶ 8)*

Therefore, serious athletes will avoid any substance that is likely to affect performance, whether it is prohibited or not.

When you use citations, you must follow APA and Harvard guidelines.

What are the guidelines?

The APA and Harvard referencing systems use the same guidelines for citations.

1   **You can use brackets to show all the details about the source. Place the citation details after the information in your essay.**

As you read each explanation, check the examples on pages 204–205.

- If you are *paraphrasing a written source*, list the author's family name and the year of publication.

    See Example 1.

  If you do not know the name of the author, use the first three or four words of the title.

    See Examples 2 and 3.

  Use the same fonts as you use in your reference entries.
  - If you are using the title of a book or website, use italics.
  - If you are using the title of an article or paper, use a regular font.

    See Examples 2, 8 and 9.

  If you do not know the date of publication, use "n.d." to show that **no date** is available.

    See Examples 3 and 4.

- If you want to cite **more than one source** for the same piece of information, place them in alphabetical order. Separate them with a semi-colon. However, if one of the sources is more important than the others, it first.

    In Example 4, both the sources have the same importance. Therefore, they are listed alphabetically. Notice how the commas and the semi-colon are used.

  Separate each part of the citation with a comma. The citation is part of the essay text. If it is placed at the end of a sentence, put the full stop after the brackets.

    See Examples 1–4 and 6.

Checkpoint

Look at Examples 1–4.

Check that you understand each one.

- If you are **paraphrasing an oral source or a personal letter**, write the person's initial and family name. Then add the words "personal communication" and the full date of the conversation.

  See Example 6.

  You should use oral sources that are knowledgeable.

  For the essay about energy drinks and sports performance, you could quote from a conversation with a sports coach or player. For other subjects, you might quote from a teacher.

  When you cite an oral source, you do not need to include it in the list of references.

Checkpoint

Look at Example 6.

Check that you understand it.

- If you are **using a direct quotation**, you should include the page number if it is available. Place it after the year of publication.

  See Example 7.

  There may be no page number if you found the quotation on an electronic database or a website. In this case, you should state the number of the paragraph. Use ¶ if possible, or write "para." and a number.

  See Examples 8, 9 and 12.

  For short direct quotations, use commas, semi-colons and full stops in the same way as for indirect quotations.

  See Examples 7–10.

> If the direct quotation is long, do not use a full stop after the brackets.
>
> See Examples 11 and 12.

Checkpoint

Look at Examples 7–9.

Check that you understand each one.

Why is "n.d." included in Example 9?

ACTIVITY 19.3   **Use brackets to cite each source.**

Time suggested:
10–15 minutes

1   Look at the essay that you used in Activities 19.1 and 19.2.
2   Place the citation details in brackets after each quotation.
   •   For each indirect quotation from a written source, use the author's family name and the year of publication.
   •   For each indirect quotation from an oral source, use the person's initial and family name, "personal communication" and the date of the conversation.
   •   For each direct quotation from a written source, use the author's family name, the year of publication, page or paragraph number.
3   Discuss your citations with a friend.

2   **You can separate the citation details so that some of them are in your essay, and some are in brackets.**

> •   If you are **paraphrasing**, you can include the author's family name as part of your essay. Place the date in brackets after the author's name.
>
> See Example 5.

> •   If you are **quoting directly**, you should include the page or paragraph number in brackets with the date.
>
> See Examples 10–12.

> You can place the brackets after the author's name or after the direct quotation.
>
> See Example 10.

- Whether you paraphrase or use a direct quotation **you can use different vocabulary**. You can introduce the author's name by using words like:
  - suggests that
  - states that
  - points out that
  - believes that
  - according to …

  See Examples 5 and 10.

  You cannot use this style if you do not know the author's name.

Checkpoint

Look at Examples 5 and 10–12.

Check that you understand each one.

ACTIVITY 19.4

Time suggested:
10–15 minutes

Separate some of the citation details.

1 Look at the essay that you used in Activity 19.3.
2 Decide which citations you want to separate.
3 Rewrite the sentences so that the author's names are not included in the brackets.
4 Discuss your citations with a friend.

Train your mind

1 Practise paraphrasing information that you read or hear.
2 Practise writing citations.
3 Use a citation for every piece of information that you find during your research.
4 Add a reference record to the list of references every time you use a citation.
5 Make your essay more interesting by separating some of the citation details.

Summarise the chapter

Quotations	An indirect quotation is … A direct quotation is …
Using short direct quotations	• Length • Position • Quotation marks?
Using long direct quotations	• Length • Position • Quotation marks?
Citations	A citation is … It is placed inside …
Reasons for using citations	• • •

When to use	Indirect quotations
	• Citation must include:
	  –
	
	  –
	
	Direct quotations
	• Citation must include:
	  –
	
	  –
	
	  –

Using brackets to show all the details	Paraphrasing a written source or personal letter • • •
	Citing more than one source for one piece of information • • Paraphrasing an oral source or personal letter • • Using a direct quotation • • Punctuation • Commas • Semi-colons • Full stops
Separating the citation details	Paraphrasing • • Direct quotations • • Useful vocabulary • • • • • This style is not suitable for …

Check your understanding

Choose the correct answers.

Check whether they are correct (page 287).

If they are not correct, read the information in this chapter again.

1   If you use an indirect quotation, you can use the exact words that another person wrote or said. True or false?

2   You should always include at least one direct quotation in an essay. True or false?

3   A paraphrase is the same as an indirect quotation. True or false?

4   If you use a long direct quotation, you should:
    a   place it in the same sentence as your writing
    b   separate it from the rest of your writing
    c   use double quotation marks.

5   A citation contains details about a source of information. It should be placed:
    a   at the beginning of an essay
    b   inside an essay
    c   at the end of an essay with the list of references.

6   You should use citations:
    a   whenever you use information or ideas that you found during your research
    b   only when you use someone else's words
    c   only if the other person's ideas are useful.

7   When you cite an indirect quotation, you should include:
    a   the author's family name, the year of publication and the page number
    b   the author's family name, "personal communication" and the page number
    c   the author's family name and the year of publication.

8   If you do not know the date of publication, you should list only the author's family name. True or false?

9   When you cite a direct quotation, you should include:
    a   the author's family name, the year of publication and the page number
    b   the author's family name, "personal communication" and the page number
    c   the author's family name and the year of publication.

10 If you cite more than one source for the same piece of information, you should separate each source with:
    a   a comma (,)
    b   a semi-colon (;)
    c   a full stop (.).

20 Using transition signals

When you have finished studying this chapter, you should be able to:

1 explain why transition signals are useful in an essay;

2 use transition signals in your writing.

Transition signals are useful writing tools.

What are transition signals?

> **transition signal** a single word or a phrase that shows how information is linked (or related)

Transition signals are single words or phrases that writers use to make their writing more effective. They show how information in different parts of a text belong together. For example, the words in the box (below) are all transition signals with the same meaning. They can be used to show how different ideas are linked (or related) to each other.

also	another	as well	furthermore	in addition	moreover

Checkpoint

What do the words in the box (above) mean?

Think of a three-letter word that has a similar meaning to all of them.

Why are they useful?

There are two main reasons for using transition signals.

Firstly, they **help the reader to understand how information in a text fits together**. The transition signals in the box above all **show similarity**. In the same way, there is a group of words that can be used to **show differences**. Some of them are listed in the box below.

although	however	in contrast
in spite of	instead of	on the other hand	though

...ese words mean?

...ink of a three-letter word that has a similar meaning to all of them.

Secondly, **transition signals help to improve writing style**. That is, they help the writing to flow more smoothly. Therefore the essay sounds more natural if it is read aloud. For example, the two texts below contain the same information. However, the writer has added transition signals to one of them.

Example 1

Most students spend a lot of time revising for their exams. Many of them do not think about their exam technique. Revision is very important. The way that you organise your time during the exam is very important.

You should plan beforehand. You will not waste time deciding what you will do and how you will do it. You will be less likely to run out of time. Planning ahead is likely to help you gain better marks.

Example 2

Most students spend a lot of time revising for their exams. However, many of them do not think about their exam technique. Although revision is very important, so is the way that you organise your time during the exam.

If you plan beforehand, you will not waste time deciding what you will do and how you will do it. In addition, you will be less likely to run out of time. Therefore planning ahead is likely to help you gain better marks.

Checkpoint

Which of the examples contains transition signals?

Which one is easiest to read?

Which one sounds best when you read it aloud?

ACTIVITY 20.1 **Identify transition signals.**

1 Re-read the example text that contains transition signals (above).
2 Find all the transition signals. Use a highlighter or a pen, or write them on a separate piece of paper.
3 Discuss your answers with a friend.

Time suggested:
5 minutes

Different transition signals are used in different ways.

How should you use them?

You can **place transition signals in different parts of a sentence**.

Some transition signals should be placed **at the beginning of a sentence**.

> For instance, "and" and "in addition" have the same meaning. You should use "in addition" to start a sentence. It is not often used in the middle of a sentence.

Some are more suitable for **inside a sentence**.

> You should never start a sentence with "and" when you are writing an academic essay.

"However" and "but" follow similar rules.

Checkpoint

Where should you place "however" and "but" in a sentence?_____

_____

_____

As well as showing similarities and differences, transition signals can **show chronological order**.

This means that they show when different actions must be done (or when they happened).

> For example, you can use words like "first", "second", "then", and "next" to explain how to do something.

These transition signals are usually placed next to an action or a thing.

> For example, if you were writing about time management for study, you could write, "The first step is to make a list of all the things that you must do."

Checkpoint

What transition signals would you use to explain:

- what happened to you yesterday? _____

_____

_____

- how to send a text message from your mobile phone? _____

_____

_____

In addition, transition signals can show **order of importance**.

In this case, you can use words like "firstly" and "secondly". These words are similar to chronological signals. However, they usually end in "–ly", and should be placed at the beginning of a sentence.

If you were writing about drunk driving, you might write: Firstly, drunk drivers are a danger to other people. Your next paragraph might begin with: Secondly, they are a danger to themselves.

Checkpoint

Think about the last essay that you wrote.

Did you use any transition signals to show order of importance?

If so, what were they? If not, what words could you have used? _____

_____

_____

Transition signals can also **show cause**.

You can use "because" to explain why something happened or why you think something.

For example, you might write:
In the South Pacific, radiation from the sun is stronger than in many other areas because the ozone layer is thinner.

"Since" can be used in the same way.

For example:
It is a good idea to use sun block and sunglasses since the sun's rays can damage your skin and eyes.

Remember that "since" can also be used when you are talking about time.

> For example:
> I have been waiting since six o'clock.

It is important to use different transition signals to **show result**.

You can do this by using words like "so" and "therefore". While you can use "so" at the beginning of a sentence, it is very useful in the middle.

> For example:
> In the South Pacific the ozone layer is thinner than in many other areas, so radiation from the sun is stronger.

"Therefore" is best placed at the beginning of a sentence.

> For example:
> Therefore it is a good idea to use sun block and sunglasses to protect your skin and eyes.

ACTIVITY 20.2   **Use the correct transition signals to show cause and result.**

Time suggested:
5–10 minutes

1   Write three sets of sentences that show cause. Use a transition signal in each set.

- _____

    _____
- _____

    _____

- _____

    _____

2   Write three sets of sentences that show result. Use a transition signal in each set.

- _____

    _____
- _____

    _____

- _____

    _____

3   Discuss your answers with a friend to make sure that the transition signals are correct.

Finally, you can use transition signals to **show examples**. The most usual words to use are:

- for example
- for instance.

If you want to **show that something happens often**, you can use:

- generally
- in general
- usually
- frequently.

If you want to **show that an example is special or unusual**, you can use:

- in particular
- especially
- sometimes
- occasionally
- from time to time.

Fifty useful transition signals

Here are 50 useful transition signals. Some of them have more than one meaning, so they appear more than once.

Words marked with * can be used inside a sentence or at the beginning. You should take care with these because they are often used differently in different parts of a sentence.

	Place at the beginning of a sentence	Place inside a sentence
To show similarity	alternatively furthermore in addition moreover of course	also another* as well as well as* or
To show difference	although* however in contrast in spite of * instead of* on the other hand	but though
To show chronological order	afterwards as long as* finally first of all lastly then when* while*	before*

	Place at the beginning of a sentence *(continued)*	Place inside a sentence *(continued)*
To show order of importance	firstly lastly in conclusion most importantly secondly thirdly	
To show cause		because* since*
To show result	as a result therefore	so* so that
To show examples	for example* for instance* generally in general in particular sometimes specifically usually*	often* especially frequently

ACTIVITY 20.3   **Practise using transition signals.**

Time suggested:
10–25 minutes

1 Add transition signals to the following paragraphs.
   • Read each paragraph carefully so that you understand it.
   • Fill each space with a transition signal from the box alongside the text.
2 Think of other transition signals with the same meaning as the ones in the boxes. You can use the list above or think of other words.
3 Discuss your answers with a friend.

Paragraph 1

There are three main reasons for using a study timetable. [1] _____ , you will avoid last-minute emergencies [2] _____ you will be better organised. [3] _____ , a timetable will enable you to make sure that you divide your time fairly between different papers. You will [4] _____ be more likely to produce better work. [5] _____ , many students do not plan their time carefully. They believe that planning their time will make their lives too regimented. [6] _____ this is a possibility, it can be prevented by having a flexible attitude.

- also
- although
- because
- however
- in addition
- most importantly

Paragraph 2

Quotations are especially important when you are writing an argumentative essay.
[1] _____ they can help to make your ideas more convincing.
[2] _____ they show the reader that you are knowledgeable
about the topic [3] _____ that other people agree with your
viewpoint. [4] _____ , a lot of direct quotations in an essay can
make it seem as though the writer has no original ideas. It is
[5] _____ a good idea to paraphrase other people's writing,
[6] _____ students who support their argument in this way gain
better marks.

- and
- firstly
- furthermore
- generally
- on the other hand
- therefore

Paragraph 3

The way that you read depends on your reason for reading. [1] _____ ,
different reading tasks require different approaches. Some tasks require careful,
intensive reading, [2] _____ others can best be achieved by
quicker, 'surface' reading. [3] _____ , if you are looking for detailed
information, you will need to read slowly and analytically. [4] _____ ,
if you need to identify only the main idea of a text, it is more efficient to read as
quickly as possible. [5] _____ you may need to read the text
several times, it will still be faster than checking every word. [6] _____ ,
this method will help you to develop faster reading skills, [7] _____
you will be able to practise reading at the same time as studying.

- but
- for example
- generally
- in contrast
- moreover
- since
- while

Paragraph 4

Many students find group work difficult. [1] _____ , they try to
avoid it. [2] _____ they understand that team skills are important
in the workplace, they still prefer to work alone. There are several reasons for this.
Working with others requires compromise. [3] _____ , it involves
accepting other people's ideas even if you don't agree with them.
[4] _____ , it is time-consuming [5] _____
it can take a while for everyone to have an opportunity to express opinions.
[6] _____ , an effective group is often more productive than the
same number of people working individually. [7] _____ , students
should be aware that well-developed group skills will make them more employable.
Learning these skills will have an important effect on their working lives.

- although
- as a result
- because
- furthermore
- in particular
- on the other hand
- therefore

Paragraph 5

The SEX formula can be used to organise paragraphs effectively. SEX stands for Statement, Explanation and eXtra details. Many writers find this formula useful. [1] _____ they identify what the paragraph is about and write a sentence describing it. This is the topic sentence – a statement which summarises the whole paragraph. ([2] _____ , they must make sure that the topic sentence is on track. [3] _____ , it must answer the response question in a direct way.) [4] _____ they explain the statement, [5] _____ the reader understands what they mean. [6] _____ , they add extra details to illustrate the explanation and make the ideas more real for the reader. This simple strategy is particularly useful for beginning writers [7] _____ it helps them to present their ideas clearly.

- because
- finally
- first
- of course
- so that
- that is
- then

ACTIVITY 20.4

Time suggested: 10 minutes

Use transition signals in your writing.

Use your own paper for this activity.

1 Look at the essay that you used for Activity 19.4, or use a different essay.
2 Check the transition signals that you have used. Make sure that they are correct.
3 Add other transition signals so that the ideas are smoothly linked.
4 Discuss your transition signals with a friend.

Train your mind

1 When you are reading, take notice of the transition signals.
2 Practise thinking of different ways to say the same thing.
3 Make sure that you know which transition signals show cause and which show result.
4 Use the table on pages 218–219 to help you decide which transition signals to use.

Summarise the chapter

Transition signals are ...	
Reasons for using	• •
Used in different ways	Place in different parts of a sentence • • Chronological order • • Order of importance • • To show cause • • To show result • • To show examples • • •

Check your understanding

Choose the correct answers.
Check whether they are correct (page 287).
If they are not correct, read the information in this chapter again.

1   Transition signals are:
   a   sentences that show the meaning of a word
   b   words or phrases that show how different information is related
   c   words that have the same meaning as other words.

2   Transition signals help the writer to understand the vocabulary in an essay. True or false?

3   You can use transition signals to:
   a   make your writing flow more smoothly
   b   repeat information in a different style
   c   plan your essay.

4   Transition signals should always be placed at the beginning of a sentence. True or false?

5   You should never start a sentence with "but" in an academic essay. True or false?

6   When you write an academic essay, you should always place "in addition" in the middle of a sentence. True or false?

7   "Lastly" is an example of a transition signal that shows:
   a   similarity and result
   b   result and order of importance
   c   chronological order and order of importance.

8   "Because" has the same meaning as:
   a   therefore
   b   since
   c   so that.

9   "In particular" has the same meaning as "in general". True or false?

10   If you want to show that something happens often, you can use:
   a   "for example", "generally" and "frequently"
   b   "in general", "sometimes" and "from time to time"
   c   "in general", "usually" and "frequently".

Answers to Activity 20.3 (pages 219–221)

Paragraph 1	Paragraph 2	Paragraph 3	Paragraph 4	Paragraph 5
1 most importantly	1 firstly	1 generally	1 as a result	1 first
2 because	2 furthermore	2 but	2 although	2 of course
3 in addition	3 and	3 for example	3 in particular	3 that is
4 also	4 on the other hand	4 in contrast	4 furthermore	4 then
5 however	5 therefore	5 while	5 because	5 so that
6 although	6 generally	6 moreover	6 on the other hand	6 finally
		7 since	7 therefore	7 because

21 Writing introductions and conclusions

Learning outcomes

When you have finished studying this chapter, you should be able to:

1 explain why introductions and conclusions are important in an essay;

2 plan and write an effective introductory paragraph;

3 plan and write an effective concluding paragraph.

The introduction and conclusion are important parts of an essay.

Why are they important?

In an essay, the introduction and conclusion have the same purposes as they do in a face-to-face conversation.

- The introduction tells the reader (or listener) about the subject that will be discussed. It gives the reader a first impression.
- The conclusion gives the reader a final impression.

When you are speaking to someone, you can check the other person's reactions and adjust what you say. However, when you write you cannot see whether the reader has understood and accepted your ideas.

- If the introduction discourages the reader, s/he may not accept the explanations in the other paragraphs. S/he may even stop reading.
- If the conclusion is poor, the reader is less likely to accept and remember the information.

Therefore, you must make sure that the introduction and conclusion are well written and clearly expressed.

When should you write them?

It is a good idea to write the introduction and conclusion *after* you have written the body of the essay. Many people find introductions difficult because they try to write them before they know what the rest of the essay contains. If you are using a computer for writing, it is easy to add the introduction near the end of the writing process.

The introduction introduces the subject.

How should you develop an introduction?

You should begin by thinking about the end of the paragraph.

You should do this because the thesis statement is usually placed, unchanged, at the end of the introduction. In this position, it is most likely to make a strong impression on the reader. If it is placed at the beginning of the paragraph, or 'buried' in the middle, the reader may not easily remember it.

    The thesis statement is the most important part of the introduction. It tells the reader about the subject of the essay and the writer's point of view.

Suppose that you were writing an essay about whether biological methods should be used for pest control. The thesis statement might be:
Biological pest control is preferable to other control methods.

The rest of the introductory paragraph must help the reader to understand the thesis statement.

There are several ways to organise the beginning of the introduction.

You can introduce the subject straightaway, perhaps adding a fact that the reader should know.

The first sentence of the introduction might be:
While biological methods of pest control are generally successful, their use is often controversial.

You might explain why the subject is important.

You might write:
Pest control has been an important issue in this country since the end of the 19th century.
or
Pests cause expensive damage to the environment and to the economy.

You might use an interesting quotation about the subject. If you do this, you should use a knowledgeable source and include an accurate citation.

You might include a quotation from a scientific journal:
While biological control methods have generally been successful, "their use triggered public outcry about animal welfare and the risk to other species" (Nowak, 2004, p. 50).

After you have introduced the subject, you should add a little more information.

You might write about the different opinions that people have about the subject.

For example:
Some people prefer physical methods of control, like trapping, because they do not affect the environment. Some consider that chemical methods offer a faster solution. Others believe that biological control is more effective In the long term

Sometimes, you might include a very short summary of the body of the essay. This is less interesting than other introductions. However, some teachers prefer it because it helps them to mark the essay quickly.

For instance:
Biological control is more effective than using other methods. It also has fewer environmental side effects.

Do not just repeat the topic sentences. If you include too much information in the introduction, you will have nothing to write about in the body of the essay. You should also avoid using obvious statements like: In this essay I will make three points.

When you have finished the introductory paragraph, check that your writing leads smoothly to the thesis statement. You might add some transition signals to improve the flow of words.

Checkpoint

Suppose you were writing an essay about the disadvantages of biological pest control. What information could you include in the introduction? _____

_____

_____

_____

_____

ACTIVITY 21.1   **Develop an introductory paragraph.**

Time suggested:
20–30 minutes

For this activity, use an essay that you are writing.
- It could be one that you worked on in Chapters 17–20, or a different one.
- You must have completed writing the body of the essay before you begin this activity.

1 Think of an interesting first sentence. Use one of:
   - a fact that the reader should know
   - an explanation of why the subject is important
   - an interesting quotation.
2 Add more information. Use one of:
   - different opinions about the subject
   - a quick summary of the body of the essay.
3 Place the thesis statement at the end of the paragraph.
4 Add transition signals.
5 Check that the paragraph flows smoothly.
6 Discuss your paragraph with a friend.

The conclusion makes the essay complete.

How should you develop a conclusion?

It is often a good idea to begin by showing that the essay is almost finished.

If you use a transition signal, your reader will understand that it is important to read the paragraph carefully.

For instance, you could write:
- In conclusion
- Therefore
- In summary

You might decide to refer to the thesis statement at the beginning of the paragraph. This will help the reader to remember what the whole essay is about, especially the writer's point of view. You should use a paraphrase of the statement that you made in the introduction.

The first sentence of your conclusion might be:
In conclusion, biological control has considerable advantages over other methods.

This has the same meaning as the original thesis statement, but it is different enough to be interesting.

You might summarise the main points of the body.
If you have already done this in the introduction,
you must use different words.

You might write:
Therefore, biological control should be our preferred method because it is more effective and environmentally friendly than other methods.

You could use this sentence instead of the paraphrased thesis statement.

The middle of the paragraph should contain some explanation.

You could place the summary of the body here, or you might suggest further action or research.

For example:
It is important that everyone understands the advantages of biological control.

You must take care not to introduce any new information. Your aim is to make your reader satisfied with your explanations. You cannot do this if you add new ideas.

The last sentence in the conclusion must show that the essay has been completed.

You might refer to the thesis statement here.

However, if you did this at the beginning of the paragraph, it would be boring to repeat it.

You might offer a challenge to the reader, or suggest further action.

You might write something like:
- It is up to everyone to become informed about this issue.
or
- We cannot expect to improve the situation unless we take advantage of the latest research in this area.

You should make sure that the your final statement is short and clear. If it is too long or vague, the reader will not be convinced.

Checkpoint

Suppose you were writing an essay about the disadvantages of biological pest control.

What information could you include in the conclusion? _____

_____

_____

_____

_____

ACTIVITY 21.2

Time suggested:
20–30 minutes

Develop a concluding paragraph.

For this activity, use the essay that you worked on in Activity 21.1.
1 Decide how you will begin the conclusion. Use a transition signal.
2 Add one of:
   • a paraphrase of the thesis statement
   • a short summary of the main points in the body of the essay.
3 Add more information. Use one of:
   • a short summary of the body, if you have not already used it
   • a suggestion for further action or research.
4 Add a final statement. Use one of:
   • a paraphrase of the thesis statement, if you have not already used it
   • a challenge to the reader
   • a suggestion for further action.
5 Check that the paragraph flows smoothly.
6 Discuss your paragraphs with a friend.

Train your mind

1 Write the introduction and conclusion after the body of an essay.
2 Place the thesis statement at the end of the introduction.
3 Practise paraphrasing so that you can write similar information in different ways.
4 Always check that you have not introduced new information in the conclusion.

Summarise the chapter

Introduction and conclusion	• Purposes: • Importance: • When to write:
Developing an introductory paragraph	Place at beginning • • • Place in middle • • • Warning Place at end Final check •
Developing a concluding paragraph	Place at beginning • • • Place in middle • • Warning Last sentence • • •

► Check your understanding ○

Choose the correct answers.

Check whether they are correct (page 287).

If they are not correct, read the information in this chapter again.

1 The introduction and the conclusion have the same purpose. True or false?

2 If the introduction is poor, the reader:
   a will not understand what the essay is about
   b will be very bored
   c will not know anything about pest control.

3 The best place for the thesis statement is:
   a at the beginning of the essay
   b at the end of the essay
   c at the end of the introduction.

4 You should never include a quotation in the introduction. True or false?

5 The introductory paragraph should include:
   a important background information that the reader should know
   b the reasons why pest control is important
   c both of the above.

6 The introduction can sometimes include a summary of the topic sentences. True or false?

7 The conclusion helps the reader to:
   a learn new information about the subject
   b remember how to use transition signals
   c understand the writer's point of view.

8 It is often a good idea to use a transition signal at the beginning of the concluding paragraph. True or false?

9 When you write a conclusion, you should include a paraphrase of the thesis statement. True or false?

10 The last sentence of your essay should:
   a paraphrase all the topic sentences
   b suggest action that the reader should do
   c be short and clear
   d all of the above.

SECTION

7

Editing

This section discusses what you need to do when you check the first draft. It suggests ways to check the content of your essay. It also explains how to make sure that your writing is organised in a logical way.

Chapter 22   Checking content and structure

22 Checking content and structure

Learning outcomes

When you have finished studying this chapter, you should be able to:

1. explain why editing is important;
2. explain how to check the content of the first draft of your essay;
3. explain how to check the structure of your essay.

Editing is an important part of writing.

Why is editing important?

Editing can help you learn more. If you examine your first draft carefully, you will often understand more about the essay subject. You will realise more clearly how different ideas and pieces of information fit together.

Editing can make your essay easier to understand. If you edit carefully, your essay is more likely to answer the question effectively. All the information and ideas will be relevant. Your explanations will be clear and well organised.

If your essay is part of an assignment, editing can help you get better marks. Your teacher is more likely to give you a good grade if your essay is on track and easy to understand.

What should you do when you edit?

When you edit your first draft, you should do two things:

1. check the content of your essay
2. make sure the structure is clear and logical.

While this sounds very simple, it is quite time-consuming and needs a lot of concentration.

You should allow enough time to edit thoroughly. It is a good idea to put your essay away for a while after you have finished the first draft. If possible, allow two or three days (or at least overnight) before starting to edit. If you do this, you will find it easier to see any problems that need correcting.

Think about the last essay that you wrote.

How much time did you spend editing?

What did you do at the editing stage?

Was your editing effective? _____

_____

_____

◀---

When you edit, you should check the content of your essay.

How should you check the content?

You can ask five questions to help you check the content of your essay.

1 Is the essay **on track**?
2 Have you included **all information** that is relevant?
3 Have you given **clear explanations**?
4 Have you used **correct vocabulary**?
5 Have you made sure there is **no plagiarism**?

You can use a mnemonic to help you remember these questions:

> Odd Tea And Ice-cream Can Easily Confuse Very Naughty People
>
> stands for
>
> On Track
>
> All Information
>
> Clear Explanations
>
> Correct Vocabulary
>
> No Plagiarism

If you want to, make up your own mnemonic to help you remember the editing questions.

_____

_____

◀---

1   OT: Is the essay On Track?

- **Check that you have understood the question correctly.**

  Suppose that your essay is about whether or not people should pay for medical treatment. The essay question might be:
  Is the funding of medical treatment a government or individual responsibility? Justify your answer.

  Look at the analysis of the question, that you made when you were planning.

  In this question, your analysis should contain three key ideas:
  - The **subject** of the essay is medical treatment.
  - Your **point of view** will be about who should pay for it.
  - You must also **explain the reasons** for your opinion.

  If you notice some gaps in the original analysis, you should change it. Use the new analysis to check the first draft.

See Chapter 6, pages 62–66, for information about analysing essay questions.

ACTIVITY 22.1

Check your analysis of an essay question.

1   Begin to edit an essay that you are writing.
2   Look at the essay question and the analysis that you made when you began to plan.
3   Make any necessary changes.
4   Discuss your answers with a friend.

Time suggested:
5–10 minutes

- **Check that the essay outline is on track.**
  Make sure that the thesis statement is clear and relevant.

  In this example, the essay 'question' is actually a question. (Sometimes it is a statement or a quotation.) Therefore, the thesis statement must answer it in a clear and direct way. Your thesis statement might be one of the following:
  - The government should be responsible for funding medical treatment.
  - The funding of medical treatment is an individual responsibility.

  Check that the response questions cover every part of the essay question and thesis statement.

  For example, one of the response questions might be: Why should the government (or individuals) pay for medical treatment?

Make sure that the topic sentences answer the response questions in a direct way.

You should be able to answer the response question, by saying "because" and adding the topic sentence.

Make sure that together the topic sentences answer all the response questions.

See Chapter 8 (pages 79–87) for information about keeping on track.

ACTIVITY 22.2

Time suggested:
5–10 minutes

Check your essay outline.

1 Look at the outline for the essay that you began editing in Activity 22.1.
2 Make sure that:
   - the thesis statement is clear and relevant
   - the response questions cover every part of the essay question and thesis statement
   - the topic sentences answer the response questions in a direct way
   - together the topic sentences answer all the response questions.
3 Make any necessary changes.
4 Discuss your outline with a friend.

- Check the topic sentences that you have used in the first draft. Sometimes, writers change the topic sentences so that they are different from the outline. Perhaps a different sentence fitted into the essay better. Perhaps they forgot to keep using the outline.

  For example:
  - One of the topic sentences in the outline might be: Every person has control over keeping fit and healthy.
  - In the first draft, the topic sentence was changed to: Keeping fit and healthy is an individual responsibility.

If you have changed the topic sentences, check that they still answer the response questions in a direct way.

- In this case, the topic sentence in the first draft means almost the same as the one in the outline. It still answers the response question in a direct way. So, you do not need to make any changes.

See Chapter 8, pages 82–83, for information about topic sentences.

ACTIVITY 22.3

Time suggested:
5–10 minutes

Check the topic sentences in your first draft.

1 Look at the first draft of the essay that you began editing in Activities 22.1 and 22.2.
2 Check that the topic sentences are the same as the ones in the essay outline.
3 If they are different, check that:
   • they have the same meaning
   • they answer the response questions in a direct way.
4 Make any necessary changes.
5 Discuss your sentences with a friend.

2 AI: Have you included All the Information that is relevant?

• **Look at the notes from your research.**
  Check that you have used every piece of relevant information.

> For instance, your notes might include information about medical problems caused by industrial pollution. This is an important point that should be included in your essay.

Make sure that each piece of information is in the right place.

• Information about illnesses caused by industrial pollution should be placed in a paragraph about government responsibilities.
• Information about keeping fit belongs in a paragraph about individual responsibilities.

See Chapter 17, pages 180–182, for information about using your notes and essay outline together.

ACTIVITY 22.4

Time suggested:
15–20 minutes

Check that you have included all relevant information.

1 Look at the first draft of the essay that you used in Activities 22.1–22.3.
2 Look at the notes that you made when you were researching.
3 Check that all the relevant information in your notes has been included in the first draft.
4 Check that each piece of information is in the right place.
5 Make any necessary changes.
6 Discuss what you did, with a friend.

3   CE: Have you given Clear Explanations?

- **Check that you have explained the reasons for your ideas.**
  Every idea should have an explanation that includes why you think in that way.

  > The paragraph about industrial pollution should explain *why* it is a government responsibility. For example, it might say that individuals do not have control of keeping the environment clean. The government is responsible for the regulations that control industrial pollution.

- **Check that you have used the KISS principle.**
  Make sure that the explanations are concise. Do not use unnecessary words.

  > Change any sentences that repeat ideas or contain clichés.

  > Use sentences with a maximum of about 20 words. You have to think carefully when you do this. You cannot just put full stops anywhere in the sentences. Sometimes you will have to change your explanation.

See Chapter 17, pages 182–185, about explaining clearly.

ACTIVITY 22.5

Time suggested: 15–20 minutes

Check that your explanations are clear.

1 Look at the first draft of the essay that you used in Activities 22.1–22.4.
2 Make sure that the explanations are clear.
   - If you are not sure, read the essay aloud to yourself, or ask a friend to read it.
3 Check that you have used the KISS principle.
   - make sure that there are no unnecessary words
   - check the length of the sentences.
4 Make any necessary changes.
5 Discuss what you did, with a friend.

4   CV: Have you used Correct Vocabulary?

- **Make sure that all the words are used correctly.**
  Use a dictionary to check the meaning of any words that you are not sure of.

  > Many students are confused about words that sound almost the same, for example:
  > - "alternate" and "alternative"
  > - "extreme" and "excessive"
  > - "interesting" and "interested"
  >
  > It is a good idea to check words that you do not often use, even if you think you know their meaning.

- **If you are writing an argumentative essay, check that you have used persuasive language.** Make sure that it is not exaggerated. Remember that it must be supported with reasons.

> You might write something like:
> The government has a moral duty to pay for medical treatment for people who were born with a disability.
> You should follow this statement by explaining why you think this.

See Chapter 17, pages 182–188, about vocabulary.

ACTIVITY 22.6

Time suggested:
10–15 minutes

Check that you have used correct vocabulary.

1 Look at the first draft of the essay that you used in Activities 22.1–22.5.
2 Make sure that you have used words correctly.
   - Check the meanings of any technical words.
   - Check words that you do not usually use.
   - If you are not sure, use a dictionary.
3 If your essay is argumentative:
   - check that you have used persuasive language
   - make sure that you have added a reason for every idea.
4 Make any necessary changes.
5 Discuss with a friend.

5 **NP: Have you made sure there is No Plagiarism?**

- **Check that you have used your own words.**
  Look at every piece of information that you found when you were researching.

> If you have copied any words, you should either:
> - rewrite the sentence so that you explain the idea in your own words
> or
> - use quotation marks and a citation to show that you are using a direct quotation.

- **Check there is a citation for every piece of information that you found when you were researching.**
  Of course, every direct quotation should have a citation. However, the indirect quotations must also be cited.

> Suppose that you found some details about how much the government spends on hospitals each year. If you did not use the exact words of the text that you found, you must still use a citation. In this case, your sentence would look like this:
> The government spends more than $4800 million each year on hospital care (Statistics New Zealand, 2005).

> • Check that the citations are correct.
> If a citation is not correct, your reader will not be able to check it.

See Chapter 19 (pages 201–212) for information about avoiding plagiarism and using citations.

ACTIVITY 22.7

Time suggested:
10–15 minutes

Check that you have not plagiarised.

1 Look at the first draft of the essay that you used in Activities 22.1–22.6.
2 Make sure that you have used your own words.
3 Check that there is a citation for every piece of information that you found.
4 Check that every citation is correct.
5 Make any necessary changes.
6 Discuss what you did, with a friend.

You must also check the essay structure.

How should you check the structure?

You can use four questions to check the structure of your essay.
1 Is every **paragraph** well organised?
2 Are the paragraphs in a **logical order**?
3 Have you used **transition signals**?
4 Does the **list of references** match the citations?

Checkpoint

Think of a mnemonic to help you remember these four questions _____

_____

1 Is every paragraph well organised?

> Read each paragraph carefully. Make sure that it uses
> the SEX or SEX-C formula. It should contain:
> • a statement
> • an explanation
> • some extra details
> • perhaps a citation.

For example, a paragraph about hospital funding might include:

S The government already accepts responsibility for funding some medical costs.

E It subsidises doctors' fees for children and pays for public hospitals.

X For example, it spends more than $4800 million each year to maintain hospitals (Statistics New Zealand, 2005).

If a paragraph is complicated, you should use the SEXEX or SEX-C EX-C formula.

See Chapter 18, pages 192–195, about paragraph structure.

ACTIVITY 22.8   Check the paragraphs.

Time suggested: 15–20 minutes

1 Look at the essay that you used in Activities 22.1–22.7.
2 Make sure that you have used the SEX or the SEXEX formula for every paragraph, or SEX-C or SEX-C EX-C.
3 Make any necessary changes.
4 Discuss your paragraph structure with a friend.

2 **Are the paragraphs in a logical order?**

Make sure that paragraphs with similar ideas and information are placed together.

You might decide to:
- place the paragraphs about public health care together
- place the paragraphs about private health care together.

Check that they are arranged in order of importance, or reverse order of importance. If your essay is about how to do something, use chronological order.

In the example essay, paragraphs about community health and poor people would be 'stronger' than ones about wealthy individuals. Therefore, they should be placed first.

If you are writing a comparative essay, check that you have used either a whole picture or a detailed approach.

See Chapter 18, pages 196–198, about organising paragraphs in a logical order.
See Chapter 9 (pages 88–95) for information about organising comparative essays.

ACTIVITY 22.9

Time suggested:
10–15 minutes

Check the paragraphs.

1   Look at the essay that you used in Activities 22.1–22.8.
2   Make sure that the paragraphs are organised logically.
   • Check that paragraphs with similar ideas and information are near each other.
   • Check that the paragraphs are organised in order of importance (or reverse order).
   • If your essay is comparative, check whether you have used a whole picture or a detailed approach.
3   Make any necessary changes.
4   Discuss your paragraph organisation with a friend.

3   **Have you used transition signals?**

Begin by checking order of importance or chronological order.

Words like "firstly" or "the most important reason" must be placed before "secondly".

Make sure that every transition signal is used correctly.

For instance:
• Signals like "in addition", "also" and "furthermore" must be used for similar ideas.
• "However" and "on the other hand" must be used to show that an idea is different from the one before.

Take special care with transition signals that show cause and result.

See Chapter 20 (pages 213–223) about using transition signals.

ACTIVITY 22.10

Time suggested:
5–10 minutes

Check the transition signals.

1   Look at the essay that you used in Activities 22.1–22.9.
2   Check the transition signals.
   • Check order of importance or chronological order.
   • Check that the signals are used correctly.
   • If your essay is comparative, check whether you have used a whole picture or a detailed approach.
3   Make any necessary changes.
4   Discuss your transition signals with a friend

4   Does the list of references match the citations?

Every citation must match an item in the list
of references.

> The example essay contains a citation about what the government
> spends to maintain hospitals. The list of references must include a
> complete record of the source of this information.

The list of references must not contain information
about any source that has not been cited.

See Chapter 14 (pages 138–155) about recording references.

ACTIVITY 22.11

Time suggested:
10 minutes

Match the citations with the list of references.

1   Look at the essay that you used in Activities 22.1–22.10.
2   Make sure that:
   - every citation matches an item in the list of references
   - the list of references does not include any unnecessary items.
3   Make any necessary changes.
4   Discuss what you did, with a friend.

Train your mind

1   Allow enough time for editing.
2   Use a checklist to make sure that you edit thoroughly.
3   Check whether an explanation is clear by asking a friend to read it.
4   Use the computer to count words.
5   Have a dictionary by your side when you edit.

You can use a checklist to help you edit your writing.

This checklist is a useful guide to make sure that your editing is thorough and complete. It is included here instead of a summary.

Checklist

			✔ or ✗
OT	Is the essay **On Track**?	Have you understood the essay question correctly?	
		Is the essay outline on track?	
		Are the topic sentences on track?	
AI	Have you included **All the Information** that is relevant?	Have you used everything that is relevant from your notes?	
		Is every piece of information in the right place?	
CE	Have you given **Clear Explanations**?	Have you included reasons for your ideas?	
		Have you used the KISS principle for: • words? • sentences?	
CV	Have you used **Correct Vocabulary**?	Are all words used correctly?	
		Have you used persuasive language where necessary (argumentative essay)?	
NP	Have you made sure there is **No Plagiarism**?	Have you used your own words?	
		Is there a citation for every piece of information that you found?	
		Are the citations correct?	
Essay structure	Is every paragraph well organised?	Have you used the SEX or SEX-C or SEXEX or SEX-C EX-C formulae?	
		Are the paragraphs in a logical order? Are similar ideas and information placed together?	
		Have you used order of importance (or reverse order, or chronological order)?	
		Have you used a whole picture or detailed approach (comparative essays only)?	
	Have you used **transition signals**?	Are order of importance and chronological order clearly signalled?	
		Is every transition signal used correctly?	
	Does the **list of references** match the citations?	Does every citation match an item in the list of references?	
		Does the list of references have records for only those citations that were used in the essay?	

► Check your understanding

Choose the correct answers.

Check whether they are correct (page 287).

If they are not correct, read the information in this chapter again.

1   When you edit, you must make sure that grammar and punctuation are 100% correct. True or false?

2   When you edit, you should check:
    a   the information and ideas and the words that you use
    b   the information and ideas, the way that you explain them, and the words that you use
    c   your explanations and the words that you use.

3   When you edit, it is a good idea to begin by checking your analysis of the essay question. True or false?

4   You can use the TRT formula to check the structure of the essay. True or false?

5   When you check the topic sentences in your first draft, you should:
    a   check whether they match the topic sentences in the outline
    b   check whether they are written in complete sentences
    c   check whether they contain transition signals.

6   You should use your notes to make sure that you have included all the relevant information in your essay. True or false?

7   You can use the KISS principle to make sure that:
    a   your explanations are concise and your sentences are easy to read
    b   your explanations contain technical vocabulary
    c   other people enjoy reading your essay.

8   A dictionary is not useful when you are editing. True or false?

9   You should use citations for:
    a   only the indirect quotations
    b   only the direct quotations
    c   both indirect and direct quotations.

10 The list of references can include items that have not been cited in the essay. True or false?

Proof-reading

This section discusses what you need to do when you make the final check of your writing. It suggests ways to make sure that grammar, punctuation and spelling are correct. It also gives some guidelines about correcting common grammar and punctuation mistakes.

23 Checking for correctness

Proof-reading is an important part of the writing process.

What is proof-reading?

mechanical errors grammar, punctuation and spelling mistakes

Proof-reading is the stage of the writing process where you check that there are no 'mechanical' errors. This means that you make sure that grammar, punctuation and spelling are correct. As you 'polish' your writing, you produce a final copy that is ready to be presented to a reader.

Proof-reading is the last stage of the writing process. If you do it too early, you will need to proof-read again at the end anyway. Some people find and correct mechanical mistakes as they work on the content. However, they should still proof-read at the end to make sure that everything is correct.

Why is proof-reading important?

Proof-reading makes sure that your essay is as good as you can make it. You should allow enough time for proof-reading. Your reader will understand your writing more easily if the mechanics are correct.

If you are studying, proof-reading can help you get better marks. Of course, the content of your essay must be correct. Your teachers want to know what you understand, and why you think in the way that you do. However, they will often give you better marks if they do not have to struggle with incorrect grammar and spelling.

How should you proof-read?

It is a good idea to plan your time so that there is a space between editing and proof-reading. If you proof-read as soon as you have finished editing, you will still be very close to your writing. If you can, put your second draft away for a couple of days (or at least overnight). When you look at it again, you will feel less close to your writing and you will do a better job of proof-reading.

It is usually easier to **check the grammar and punctuation first**, because changing them may involve some rewriting.

Checkpoint

Think about the last essay that you wrote.

When did you proof-read? How did you do it? Did you allow enough time?

How could you have improved the proof-reading stage? _____

_____

_____

You must make sure that the grammar is correct.

What grammar should you check?

You should concentrate on checking the grammar that you have difficulty with. If your sentence structure is usually correct, there is no need to spend a lot of time checking every sentence. Similarly, if you know that you have problems with tenses, it is a good idea to spend a lot of time checking all the verbs.

While everybody has different strengths and weaknesses, there are five common grammar problems that occur in tertiary essays:

1 **Verbs and tenses**

   Different languages use different ways to show when something happened. Some use different word endings; others use different words. If your first language is very different from English, you may find it difficult to use verbs.

2 **Sentence structure**

   Some people have problems writing complete sentences or they join two sentences together with a comma. For these difficulties, your teacher may write "fragment" in the margin or "comma splice" or "run-on sentence".

3 **Articles**

   People who speak English as a first language usually use articles ("a", "an", "the") automatically, without thinking about them. However, articles are not used in some languages. Articles are important words in English, so it is important to use them correctly.

4 **Word order**

   Again, English speakers usually manage this without thinking about it. Different languages organise sentences in different ways. Word order may be a problem for you if English is not your first language.

5 **Parts of speech**

   It is important to use the correct word form. You should not use a noun in place of an adjective, or a verb instead of a noun. For example, you should be able to use "health" (noun) and "healthy" (adjective) correctly; and "practise" (verb) and "practice" (noun).

Chapter 24, pages 259–266 has more information about these grammar points.

Checkpoint

What are *your* strengths and weaknesses with grammar?

What should you spend most time checking when you proof-read?

Is the computer useful for checking grammar?

While the computer is certainly a useful tool, you should not always follow its advice.

A lot of computer software is written in America, so many of the grammar checks use American grammar 'rules'.

For example, the American rules about using "that" and "which" are not usually followed in New Zealand or Australia.

In addition, grammar 'rules' are changing all the time.

Words like "whom" are used less than before. Teachers used to insist on sentences like "I do not know to whom this pencil belongs." Now they are more likely to accept "I do not know who this pencil belongs to."

Furthermore, the computer does not always identify grammar problems correctly. Consider these examples:

In both these examples, the computer's suggestions are not correct. This is because the computer often checks small groups of words instead of looking at the whole meaning.

Original words	**Words suggested by the computer grammar check**
One person may have better research skills than the others in the group.	One person may have better research skills than the others may in the group.
You can say something like …	You can says something like …

ACTIVITY 23.1

Time suggested:
10–15 minutes

Check your grammar.

1   Use the essay that you edited when you read Chapter 22, or choose a different essay.
2   Check the grammar.
    • Spend most time on the grammar points that you identified in the last checkpoint.
    • Check other grammar points more quickly.
3   Make any necessary changes.
4   Discuss what you did, with a friend.

Check all punctuation.

Why should you check punctuation?

Correct punctuation helps to make your writing easier for the reader to understand.

Punctuation acts like a signpost for the reader.

For instance:
• Full stops show where one idea ends and another begins.
• Commas can show how ideas are linked together.
• Apostrophes show ownership.

If the punctuation is incorrect, your reader will become distracted. Instead of focussing on the information, s/he will notice the mistakes that you have made. You want your reader to concentrate on the content of the essay. S/he is unlikely to notice the punctuation if it is correct!

What punctuation should you check?

As a minimum, you should check:
• **full stops**
• **commas**
• **apostrophes.**

These are the most basic forms of punctuation. Of course, punctuation use is related to grammar. For instance, you must know about sentence structure in order to place a full stop correctly.

You might also want to check **more advanced punctuation**.

• **Quotation marks** show that the writer has used someone else's words.
• **Brackets** are used for citations, to show the author and year of a source of information. They are sometimes called parentheses.
• **Colons** show that whatever follows is strongly related to the last few words.
• **Semi-colons** are useful for breaking up long sentences and making the meaning clear.

While these are used less than basic punctuation, they are useful for more advanced writing.

You are unlikely to need exclamation and question marks in an academic essay.

- **Exclamation marks** show that something is surprising or shocking. They are not very useful in an academic essay, because you want your reader to accept your ideas easily.
- **Question marks** are not used in academic writing because your main aim is to explain or persuade. Therefore, you should use statements, not questions. If you use the TRT formula, your only questions are response questions, which do not appear in the final copy.

See Chapter 24 (pages 267–273) for information about punctuation.

Checkpoint

What punctuation can you use correctly? _____

_____

What punctuation do you need to learn to use? _____

_____

How should you check punctuation?

When you check punctuation, you should use the same process as for checking grammar and spelling.

You should concentrate especially on the areas where you have difficulty.

If you always have problems with full stops, you should check every sentence carefully. However, if your full stops are usually correctly placed, then a quick check is probably enough.

It is a good idea to check the more advanced punctuation more carefully than the basic full stops and commas.

For instance:
- You should make sure that all short quotations have quotation marks at the beginning and the end.
- You should also make sure that you use them consistently – either both single or both double quotation marks.

You should replace all apostrophes that have been used for contractions. Academic writing is usually formal, so you should use complete words.

For example:

Do not use:	**Do use:**
can't	cannot/can not
'cos	because
isn't	is not
it's	it is
shouldn't	should not
they've	they have

This means that you need to use apostrophes *only* to show ownership. Remember that you do not need an apostrophe when you use "its" to show ownership.

For example, the sentence "The government changed its taxation policy in 2005" is correct without an apostrophe.

Think carefully about suggestions from the grammar check on the computer. It is not always correct. You are the writer so you should be in control, not the computer.

ACTIVITY 23.2

Time suggested: 5–10 minutes

Check punctuation.

1 Use the essay that you began to proof-read in Activity 23.1.
2 Check the grammar.
   • Spend most time on the punctuation that you have most difficulty with.
   • Check other punctuation more quickly.
3 Make any necessary changes.
4 Discuss with a friend.

Your spelling should be correct.

Why should your spelling be correct?

You writing will be easier to understand if the spelling is correct. Consider this sentence from an essay about the importance of friendship:

In praticular, fiends enjoy each other's company.

In this sentence, the two spelling mistakes make it difficult for the reader to understand what the writer wants to say. It is not clear whether the writer means
   • "in particular" or "in practice"
   • "fiends" (devils or monsters) or "friends".

Your reader will have a better impression of your work if there are no spelling mistakes.

If a word is spelt incorrectly, it may have a different meaning even though it sounds the same. For instance, compare the differences between these sentences:

Sales are falling off.
The builder had a saw.
The ship was going to Fiji.

Sails are falling off.
The builder had a sore.
The sheep was going to Fiji.

Make sure that you also know the differences between more common sets of words, like:

* there, their, they're
* two, too, to.

It is your responsibility to make sure that the words mean what you want them to say.

How should you check your spelling?

If you are not sure about how to spell a word, **check it in a dictionary**. You can use a paper dictionary or an electronic one. There are also many good dictionaries on the internet.

You can **use the computer spell check**, but be careful how you do this. Most spell-check programs default to American spellings. This means that they use American spellings unless you change the setting. Also, they check each word separately and do not consider the meaning of the word. So, the computer will not always correct your mis-spelled word. For instance, the spell check would not find problems with any of the examples in the paragraph before last: sales/sails, saw/sore, ship/sheep, there/their/they're, two/too/to. Therefore, you must not rely on the computer to highlight all your errors. You must think about each word and decide whether the computer's advice is correct.

Checkpoint

Think of other sets of words that the computer spell check would not identify. _____

_____

_____

Make sure that your spelling is consistent.

This means that you should use the same style of spelling for the whole essay. It is a good idea to re-set the default for the computer spellcheck. If you use American English spelling for some words, you should use it for all vocabulary.

consistent spelling using the same style of spelling, e.g. New Zealand English or Australian English or United Kingdom English or American English

For instance:
- If you use "color" and "behavior", you should also use "organization", "program" and "center".
- If you use United Kingdom or Australian or New Zealand English, you must use "colour", "behaviour", "organisation", "programme" and "centre".

Generally, Australian English and New Zealand English are the same as United Kingdom English.

However, New Zealand English includes some words that are special to New Zealand, like "kumara", "tapu" and "mana". Australian English has words like "corroborree", "billabong" and "bush tucker".

Checkpoint

Think of other words that are spelled differently in different 'Englishes'.

_____

_____

It is a good idea to **identify the words that you usually have difficulty with**. Many people find that they have problems with only a small group of words. If you are one of these people, you should spend some time learning these spellings. Then you should always double-check them when you proof-read. People who say, "I always make that mistake!" are really saying that they are not interested in improving!

Checkpoint

What words do you regularly mis-spell?

- How do you overcome this problem?

or

- What could you do to overcome this problem? _____

_____

_____

ACTIVITY 23.3   **Check spelling.**

Time suggested:
10 minutes

1 Use the essay that you began to proof-read in Activities 23.1 and 23.2.
2 Check the spelling.
   - Begin by checking the words that you have most difficulty with.
   - Check other spelling by using the dictionary or the computer spell check.
3 Make any necessary changes.
4 Discuss what you did, with a friend.

It is a good idea to develop your own checklist for proof-reading.

Why do you need a personal checklist?

Everyone has different strengths and weaknesses, so it is important to develop your own checklist for proof-reading. You can use it to proof-read all your academic writing.

ACTIVITY 23.4   **Develop a personal proof-reading checklist.**

1 Look at your answers to the checkpoints in this chapter.
2 Record them in the table below.

Time suggested:
5–10 minutes

You can use this table to remind you what you need to check. You can also use it to help you proof-read. As you check each aspect of your writing, place ticks and crosses in the *Self-check* column. You can ask a friend to proof-read for you by using the *Peer check* column.

		Self-check	Peer check
Grammar			
Punctuation			
Spelling			

Train your mind

1   Allow enough time for proof-reading.
2   Check grammar, punctuation and spelling.
3   Identify your weaknesses and concentrate on them.
4   Think carefully about the grammar and spelling suggestions from the computer.

Summarise the chapter

Proof-reading is ...	
Importance	
Timing	
Method	
Checking grammar	**Grammar points** • Verbs and tenses • Sentence structure • Articles • Word order • Parts of speech **Computer grammar check** • Grammar 'rules' • Identifying grammar problems

Checking punctuation	Basic punctuation
	• Full stops
	• Commas
	• Apostrophes
	More advanced punctuation
	• Quotation marks
	• Brackets
	• Colons
	• Semi-colons
	Often unnecessary
	• Exclamation marks
	• Question marks
Checking spelling	• Dictionary use
	• Computer spell check
	• Being consistent

Check your understanding

Choose the correct answers.

Check whether they are correct (page 287).

If they are not correct, read the information in this chapter again.

1   When you proof-read, you should check that all the information in your essay is correct. True or false?

2   Proof-reading should be done:
   a   as soon as you have completed the outline
   b   when you have completed the first draft
   c   after you have finished writing.

3   You should allow enough time for proof-reading because:
   a   it will help you to make sure that the essay is easy to read and understand
   b   it is more important than the content
   c   it is the most important stage of the writing process.

4   When you proof-read, you should:
   a   check every word very carefully
   b   identify your weaknesses and concentrate on them
   c   check your strengths before you check your weaknesses.

5   The grammar in different languages:
   a   is often organised differently from English grammar
   b   never has the same order as English
   c   always uses articles.

6   The computer is a useful proof-reading tool, but it is sometimes not correct. True or false?

7   If your punctuation is correct, your reader:
   a   will be able to concentrate on understanding the content
   b   will spend time looking for mistakes
   c   will find your essay very interesting.

8   You should never use apostrophes in an essay. True or false?

9   You should check your spelling carefully because:
   a   words that sound the same often have different meanings
   b   the computer spell check is never correct
   c   New Zealand and Australian English use the same spelling as American English
   d   all of the above.

10 A personal checklist is useful for proof-reading because:
   a   you can photocopy it and keep it in your bag
   b   your strengths and weaknesses may not be the same as other people's
   c   your friends can look at it and use it too.

24 Troubleshooting grammar and punctuation problems

Note:

This chapter is a troubleshooting guide. Only the most common problems are explained, and the explanations are brief.

Therefore, there are no learning outcomes because you should use this chapter in a different way from the others. Instead of studying the whole chapter, you should concentrate on the areas where you need to improve.

- If your writing has been marked, you can use the troubleshooting guide below to identify find your problem.
- If you have already identified the problem, you can go straight to the correct section.

If you have a lot of difficulties, you should find help. There are many good English grammar books with clear explanations and exercises. In addition, many universities and polytechnics offer extra help with grammar and punctuation.

Troubleshooting guide

Teacher's comments	Where to look for help	Teacher's comments	Where to look for help
a/an	3 Articles	tense?	1 Verbs and tenses
comma splice	6 Full stops	the	3 Articles
fragment	1 Verbs and tenses 2 Sentence structure	use a noun/adjective /verb/adverb	5 Parts of speech
incomplete sentence	1 Verbs and tenses 2 Sentence structure	when did this happen?	1 Verbs and tenses
incorrect punctuation	6 Full stops 7 Commas 8 Apostrophes 11 Colons 12 Semi-colons	*word is crossed out and replaced*	5 Parts of speech
		word is underlined	5 Parts of speech
		wrong order	4 Word order
run-on sentence	6 Full stops	wrong tense	1 Verbs and tenses
parentheses	9 Brackets	wrong word form	5 Parts of speech
present or past?	1 Verbs and tenses	⌐¬	4 Word order
punctuation needed	6 Full stops 7 Commas 8 Apostrophes 11 Colons 12 Semi-colons	.	6 Full stops
		,	7 Commas
		'	8 Apostrophes
		( )	9 Brackets
		" "	10 Quotation marks
		' '	10 Quotation marks
sentence structure	1 Verbs and tenses 2 Sentence structure	:	11 Colons
show ownership	8 Apostrophes	;	12 Semi-colons

1   Verbs and tenses

Many people find verbs difficult. The way a verb is formed can be completely different in different languages.

verb a word or phrase that explains what someone or something does; or shows that someone or something exists

A verb is a word or phrase that explains what someone or something does.

For example, in the sentence "The woman wrote an essay", "wrote" is a verb.

If you have a problem with verbs, your teacher's comments may include:
- verb missing
- fragment
- incomplete sentence
- sentence structure
- complete verb needed.

Sometimes a verb shows that someone or something exists instead of *doing* something.

- In "I am 25 years old", "am" is a verb because it explains that someone exists.
- In "The desk is in the office", "is" is a verb.

In English, every sentence must contain a **complete verb**.

A complete verb makes sense if you place someone or something in front of it.

For example, consider the sentence: "Acting on behalf of the whole community, the government is responsible for collecting taxes." If you say "the government is ...", the words make sense. Therefore "is" is a complete verb.

You cannot do this if a verb is not complete.

"Acting" and "collecting" are not complete verbs. They do not make sense if you put something in front of them. You cannot say "the government acting" or "the government collecting".

Sometimes a complete verb uses more than one word.

For example, in the sentence "the agent was representing everyone in the team", "was representing" is a complete verb.

Checkpoint

1   Look at one of the sample essays in this book and identify the complete verbs.

2   Do *you* have difficulties with verbs? If so, how can you solve this problem?

Most academic writing uses the present tense. However, sometimes you need to write about the past or the future.

We use tenses to show when something happens (or happened).

> If you have problems with tenses, your teacher might write:
> - present or past?
> - when did this happen?

tense a verb form that shows when something happens (or happened)

Verbs are pronounced and spelt differently for different tenses.

> For example, the verb "to buy" has several different forms. Here are some of them:
> - (I) am buying
> - (I) buy
> - (I) was buying
> - (I) bought
> - (I) will buy
> - (The gift) was bought
> - (The gift) will be bought
> - (The gift) is bought

If you have difficulty with tenses, you should check every verb in your essay. Ask yourself "What time am I writing about – past, present or future?" Then choose which tense to use. You can use transition signals to help you.

> For example, you might use words like:
> - at present
> - now
> - in the past
> - ten years ago.

Checkpoint

1   Look at one of the sample essays in this book and identify the tenses.

2   Do *you* have difficulties with tenses? If so, how can you solve this problem?

2   Sentence structure

Some people have problems writing complete sentences.

sentence a group of words that makes sense alone and contains a complete verb

This problem often happens because they do not make sure that every sentence contains a complete verb.

If you have this difficulty, your teacher's comments might be:
- fragment
- incomplete sentence.

compound sentence a sentence with two related parts

Sometimes, people treat a compound sentence like two simple sentences. A compound sentence has two parts that are related.

For example, look at the sentence: Although carrots are good for health, many children prefer ice-cream.
- This compound sentence contains two ideas that are related.
- It has two complete verbs ("are" and "prefer").

Sometimes, one of the parts in a compound sentence makes sense on its own.

In this case, you could use "Many children prefer ice-cream" on its own. It contains a complete verb and it is a complete sentence.

Sometimes, one part of a compound sentence cannot be used alone. Even if it contains a complete verb, it does not make sense without the other half of the sentence.

"Although carrots are good for health" cannot be used on its own. It makes sense only if it is joined to the other half of the sentence.

▶

In this example, "although" is a transition signal that must be used as part of a compound sentence.

Some transition signals should always be used as part of a compound sentence, especially if they are placed near a verb:

- after
- although
- because
- but
- since
- so that
- though
- when (if not part of a question)
- while.

3   Articles

Articles tell the reader whether you are talking about something special or something general; "the", "a", and "an" are all articles.

If you have problems with articles, your teacher might write:
- "the" or "a" or "an"(with an arrow / to show where it should be placed).

"The" is a definite article. You should use it to show that you are talking about something specific.

For example, suppose that you wrote:
"The government has changed its policy."

In this sentence, you would not mean any government. You would be talking about a particular government. The reader would know which government you meant. You probably mentioned the government in an earlier sentence.

> definite article "the"; used to talk about something specific

- You can use "the" to make a general statement. In this case, you should use a singular noun.

You might write:
"**The book** is a convenient way to record information because it is easy to carry."

This is a statement about books in general; it is not about any special book.

- You can also make a general statement by not using "the". In this case, you should use a plural noun.

For example, you might write:
"**Laptop computers** are convenient because they are portable."

indefinite article "a" or "an"; used for general examples

- "A" and "an" are indefinite articles. You should use them for general examples.

> For instance, you might write:
> "A computer is a useful writing tool."
> In this case, you would not mean a special computer or a special writing tool.

If the noun begins with a vowel (a, e, i, o, u), you should use "an" instead of "a".

> For example:
> A mobile phone can be useful in **an emergency**.

You cannot use "a" and "an" when you are talking about more than one thing.

Checkpoint

1   Look at one of the sample essays in this book and identify the articles.

2   Do *you* have difficulties with articles? If so, how can you solve this problem?

4   Word order

Every language uses a particular order for words in a sentence or phrase. First-language speakers often use the correct order without thinking about it.

If English is not your first language, you might need to learn some "rules" to help you.

> If you have this sort of difficulty, your teacher's comments might be:
> - wrong order
> - ⌐⌐

If you are using a lot of detail to describe something, the adjectives should *usually* appear in this order:

- opinion
- physical information
- colour
- condition
- origin
- material
- type
- purpose.

Examples:
- an **interesting non-fiction** book (opinion and type)
- a **large, square** box (opinion and physical information)
- a **long blue** pencil (opinion and colour)
- the **small red cotton** T-shirt (opinion, colour and material)
- the **South African netball** team (origin and type)
- the **best medical** information (opinion and type)
- the **torn shoulder** muscle (condition and type)

It is important to remember that sometimes this word order can be changed.

Do *you* have difficulties with word order? If so, how can you solve this problem?

Many people have difficulties with using "only" and "really" correctly.

> If you have this problem, your teacher might draw an arrow to show where the word should be moved to.

They often place "only" immediately before a verb. However, its place in a sentence depends on what you want to say.

> Look at the table below for examples.

"Really" follows the same patterns as "only". However, it is used in two places:
- at the beginning or end of a sentence
- with a verb.

> Look at the examples in the table below.

Using "only" and "really"	
Example	**Explanation**
Only the last sentence refers to the thesis statement.	The last sentence is special. No other sentence is about the thesis statement.
The last sentence **only** refers to the thesis statement	That is all it does. It is not very much.
The last sentence refers **only** to the thesis statement.	The last sentence is not about anything else except the thesis statement.
The last sentence refers to the **only** thesis statement.	There is one thesis statement, not several.
Really, I do not want to go to the beach.	I want you to believe that I am telling the truth.
I do not want to go to the beach **really**. or I do not **really** want to go to the beach.	I do not have very strong feelings, but I would prefer to go somewhere else.

Checkpoint

Do *you* have difficulties with using "only" or "really" correctly?

If so, how can you solve this problem?

5   Parts of speech

In English, words have different forms, depending on what they do in a sentence.

For example, "interested" and "interesting" are used differently. So are "health" and "healthy".

This is sometimes a problem for second-language speakers because they are used to different grammar.

If this is one of your difficulties, your teacher might:
- cross out a word and replace it
- write "use a noun" or "use an adjective" in the margin
- underline the word that is wrongly used.

When you write, you should think carefully about using the correct parts of speech, so that your meaning is clear. Sometimes, a word 'family' has more than one form of adjective.

For instance:
- You should use "**interested**" to describe a person who is concentrating on something. For example, you could write: I am **interested** in Hip Hop.
- You should use "**interesting**" to describe something that is worth examining. For example, you could write: Hip Hop is more **interesting** than jazz.

You should also make sure that you know the difference between the word form for nouns and adjectives.

For example, suppose that you were writing an essay about health. You should remember that "health" is a noun, and "healthy" is an adjective. Therefore, you should write about "good **health**" and "**healthy** food".

Checkpoint

Do *you* have difficulties with using parts of speech correctly?

If so, how can you solve this problem?

6   Full stops

A full stop is a signal that the writer has reached the end of an idea. It shows the reader some suitable places to pause, or to take a breath if s/he is reading aloud.

If you have problems with full stops, your teacher will often write comments like:
* run on sentence
* comma splice
* punctuation needed
* .

If you do not use full stops, your writing will be difficult to understand because the ideas will "run together".

For example, look at this 'sentence':
The early morning is often a good time for writing many people find it a more productive time than the evening.
It contains two ideas which are not separated clearly.

Sometimes people use commas to separate ideas. However, this is not very effective, because a comma is a signal for only a very short pause.

For example:
The early morning is often a good time for writing, many people find it a more productive time than the evening.

You should use a full stop to separate each different piece of information. Begin each new sentence with a capital letter. Remember that every sentence must contain a complete verb.

The early morning is often a good time for writing. Many people find it a more productive time than the evening.

Checkpoint

Do *you* have difficulties with using full stops correctly?

If so, how can you solve this problem?

7 Commas

Commas show where small pieces of information begin and end.

They are signals that tell the reader about information that is related.

If you have problems with commas, your teacher might write comments like:
- punctuation needed
- ,

Commas are usually used to separate items in a list.
If each item contains only one word, a comma is not usually needed before the word "and".

For example:
Most children will happily eat bananas, oranges, strawberries and apples.

If some of the items contain several words, a comma before the final "and" makes the meaning clearer.

Some fruits taste good when mixed together. For instance, apple and blackberry, rhubarb and orange, and strawberry and banana are especially nice.

Commas can also be used to divide compound sentences.

For example:
Although I like bananas, I prefer mangoes.

If you are writing a complicated sentence, you can use commas to make the meaning clearer.

Look at this sentence:
You will save time if you know which fruits are in season before you decide what combination to choose.
It is not very clear whether "before you decide what combination to choose" is related to knowing about the fruit or to the fruit seasons.
It would be clearer to write:
You will save time if you know which fruits are in season, before you decide what combination to choose.

Commas are also useful when you want to separate a transition signal from the rest of the sentence.

For example:
- For instance, strawberries are at their best around Christmas time.
- However, the blackberries are not ripe until the apples are being picked.
- Lastly, it is often a good idea to make sure that the fruit is in good condition.

▾ *Checkpoint*

Do *you* have difficulties using commas correctly?

If so, how can you solve this problem?

8   Apostrophes

As academic writing is formal, there is no need to use apostrophes for contractions (informal words like "don't" and "couldn't"). In addition, you must not use apostrophes to show plurals.

> For instance, you do not need any apostrophes in this sentence:
> Different political parties have different viewpoints about tax reforms.

You *do* need to use apostrophes to show ownership.

> If you have difficulties with apostrophes, your teacher's comments might be:
> *   show ownership
> *   '

Using apostrophes is not difficult, as long as you think carefully.

First, you need to think about who or what is 'owning' something.

> For example, you might write about "the Labour governments most important tax reform". In this phrase, the tax reform belongs to the Labour government, so it is the 'owner'.

Then you must ask yourself: How is the 'owner' usually spelt? If it does not usually end with "s", you must add an apostrophe and follow it with "s".

> In this case, "government" does not usually end with "s". Therefore, you should write: The Labour government**'s** most important tax reform.

Sometimes the 'owner' already ends with "s".

> For instance, suppose that you wrote: "according to the Department of Statistics report". The Department of Statistics is the 'owner' of the report.

In this situation, you should add only an apostrophe.

> So, you would write: "according to the Department of Statistics' report".

This method is easy to use, as long as you follow the steps and ask the question.

Checkpoint

Do *you* have difficulties using apostrophes correctly?

If so, how can you solve this problem?

9   Quotation marks

You must use quotation marks if you use someone else's words in your writing.

Quotation marks are sometimes called "speech marks". They show that you have used the exact words that someone wrote or said.

If you have difficulty using quotation marks, your teacher might write them around the quoted words:
- " "

or
- ' '

If you use someone's exact words, you must place double quotation marks around them.

For example, if you were writing about the value of biological pest control, you might write:
"Biological methods have ultimately been successful" (Pockley, 2004, p. 23), although their use has often been controversial.

If the quotation follows your own words in a sentence, you should use a comma before the quotation marks, and a full stop after them.

Pockley (2004, p.23) states that, "biological methods have ultimately been successful".
In this case, you can change the first letter of the quotation to lower case.

If your quotation has another quotation inside it, you should use single quotation marks for the second one.

For example: "Sensationally, a scare ran through the media that 'myxo' was causing an emerging and fatal disease." (Pockley, 2004, p. 23)

You can also use quotation marks to show that a word or phrase has a special meaning that is unusual. When they do this, many writers prefer to use single quotation marks.

For example, you might write:

Sometimes the essay 'question' is really a statement that you have to explain.

This shows that the word "question" has a special meaning in this particular essay.

Quotation marks must always be used in pairs, either both double or both single. You cannot begin a quotation with double and end it with single.

Checkpoint

Do *you* have difficulties with using quotation marks correctly?

If so, how can you solve this problem?

10   Brackets

Brackets are used for information that supports a main idea.

Brackets are sometimes called "parentheses". They are never used for important information. However, they are helpful if you want to include a small detail that the reader needs to know.

If you have difficulties with using brackets, your teacher might write:
- parentheses
- ( )

In academic writing, their main use is with citations. You should place brackets around the details about information that you have quoted.

The examples about quotations (page 270) use brackets to show details about the author, date and page of some information.

You can place brackets around other detailed information. This might be a quick explanation of a technical word, or a direction to the reader. Do not use brackets for a large amount of information.

- You might write:
  Before you begin to write, you should analyse (examine) the essay question.
- The examples about quotations (page 270) show details about the author, date and page of some information.

Checkpoint

Do *you* have difficulties with using brackets correctly?

If so, how can you solve this problem?

11   Colons

Colons show that whatever follows is strongly related to the last few words.

If you have difficulty with colons, your teacher might write:
- punctuation needed
- incorrect punctuation
- :

A colon shows that the next few words are examples or explanations of what you have just written. If they are part of a sentence, the words that follow a colon do not have to include a complete verb.

You might write:
- Auckland's population contains a large number of different ethnic groups: Pakeha, Māori, Pasifika, Chinese, Korean and Indian.
- You should be able to use five different sorts of punctuation: full stops, commas, quotation marks, colons and semi-colons.

You can also use colons when you record a reference.
- A colon can separate two parts of a book or article title.
- When you use APA format, you should put a colon between the place of publication and the publisher's name.
You use a capital letter after a colon if it is part of a reference.

For example:
Thoreau, M. (2005). *Write on track: A guide to academic writing.* Auckland, New Zealand: Prentice Hall.

Checkpoint

Do *you* have difficulties with using colons correctly?

If so, how can you solve this problem?

12   Semi-colons

Semi-colons are useful for breaking up long sentences and making the meaning clear.

While they are used less than basic punctuation, they are useful for more advanced writing.

If you have problems using semi-colons, your teacher might make comments like:
- punctuation needed
- incorrect punctuation
- ;

You can use a semi-colon to join two small sentences that are strongly related.

In this sentence, the writer wanted to show that the two parts are closely linked:
Time planning is an essential study skill; without it, a student is unlikely to be successful.

Semi-colons can also separate items in a complicated list. They are especially helpful if some of the items contain details or explanations.

For example, this list has a lot of details:
Time planning involves organising activities that are compulsory and fixed; compulsory and flexible; voluntary and fixed; and voluntary and flexible.

Checkpoint

Do *you* have difficulties with using semi-colons correctly?

If so, how can you solve this problem?

Appendix

This section contains some additional useful material. There are five sample essays, with questions for analysis and discussion. There is a glossary which contains definitions of technical vocabulary. In addition, there are answers to the quizzes that appear at the end of each chapter.

Sample essays

Glossary

Answers to *Check your understanding* quizzes

Sample essays

Sample 1: Simple expository essay

The downside of overseas travel

Travel has never been quicker or cheaper. It is now easier to travel, and so easier to visit and understand the rest of the world. However, this new-found opportunity has definite disadvantages. Overseas travel is not always beneficial.

Firstly, overseas travel can harm your bank balance. Tickets are expensive. Flying is perhaps the dearest way to take a trip. Even though it is sometimes possible to buy cheap tickets, it is not always easy to plan far enough ahead. Sea journeys, which used to be cheaper, are now limited to expensive cruises. Trains are often as costly as flying, and you cannot use them to go overseas. If you decide to travel independently, you face the costs of petrol and car-hire when you arrive at your destination. In addition, accommodation costs are high – even if you stay in budget lodgings. Day-to-day expenses are also higher than if you stayed at home.

Secondly, travelling by plane over long distances is often uncomfortable and tiring. The problems begin with waiting in line to check in your luggage; then you must wait to clear customs and immigration. Once on board, the constant vibration of the engines causes drowsiness. Unless you travel first or business class, you will find air travel cramped and uncomfortable. There is not enough leg room, and you cannot sleep properly because you have to stay sitting up. Furthermore, sitting in one position for a long time is hazardous to health – deep vein thrombosis and dehydration are two possible dangers. Air-sickness is another common problem, as is lifting heavy luggage.

Furthermore, overseas travel can be dangerous. While there are strict regulations which govern the standard of aircraft maintenance, accidents do happen. We occasionally hear of mid-air crashes, engine failure or other problems. In addition, there is always the threat of high-jacking. This problem has worsened as activists have realised the opportunities that are available for them to make their wishes known.

In addition, if you do not know another language, you may not learn much about the places you are visiting. In many really interesting places, the ones that are completely different from your country, people will not know your language. Also, in some countries the writing is in a different script. If you cannot read, you cannot easily find information about reaching a destination, or about the things you should see. If you cannot speak some local language, people will not be able to help you or explain things to you.

Finally, sightseeing in foreign countries may not help you to understand other cultures. Of course, seeing interesting buildings and monuments will give you some basic factual information about a country's history. You can look at the scenery and learn a little about its geography. You can find out about the food by looking in the shops and markets. You can even read about the culture in guide books. However, the real 'heart' of a country is found through meeting its people. They are the ones who can tell you the stories that accompany the history. They can explain about the different seasons and festivals, and give you background information about what you observe. They can show you how to cook traditional dishes. Only through spending time with the local people can you begin to understand what and how they think. Sightseeing tours do not always make this possible.

In conclusion, while overseas travel certainly has many advantages, it also has its downside. If you want to travel, you need to be aware of the potential difficulties. Then you can plan to meet and overcome them, so that you gain maximum benefit from your time overseas.

Questions to think about and discuss

1   What is the thesis statement of this essay? Where has the writer placed it?
2   What are your response questions?
3   Where has the writer placed the topic sentences? Are they placed consistently?
4   Does each topic sentence help to answer the response questions *in a direct way*?
5   Has the writer used the SEX (or SEXEX) formula in every paragraph?
6   Do the topic sentences together give a clear and complete answer to the response questions?
7   Have the paragraphs been placed in a logical order? How do you think the writer decided which order to use?
8   How has the writer used transition signals to link ideas?
9   Is the introduction effective? Does it lead smoothly to the thesis statement?
10 Is the conclusion effective? How does it show the reader that the essay is finished?
11 What is your overall impression of this essay?

Sample 2: Simple expository essay

The importance of inactivity

Many people believe that they should work hard all the time. They do not want others to think that they are lazy. However, too much work causes stress and lowers resistance to infection. It is important to make sure that you have time to relax. Sometimes it is all right to do nothing.

Doing nothing for a while will often help you to work better later. If you have been working very hard, you will be unable to work efficiently. Sitting and chatting, or just listening to music, will help you to recover more quickly. A short sleep may also be helpful. Afterwards, you will feel refreshed and will be able to concentrate again.

It may be a good idea to do nothing if you are feeling stressed. It is true that, for some people, being active helps them to forget their worries. They may be able to 'lose' themselves while playing a sport or doing some craft work. However, many people prefer to take it easy on the beach or in a peaceful park. Your mental health will improve if you feel relaxed.

Sometimes, you should do nothing if you are a little unwell. You will recover more quickly if you stay at home and rest, instead of going to work. In addition, your co-workers will not be pleased if they catch your infection. If your illness is a minor one, you might not even need to take any medication.

Sometimes a problem will be solved without any action from you. This is particularly true in times of change. For example, suppose that you have moved to a new country. If the culture is very different, you will probably feel homesick. You may find the food strange and you will miss your family and friends. This is a very normal feeling for people who travel. However, if you go home straight away you will probably not improve the situation. This problem will become less stressful as you become more used to your new environment.

If a problem belongs to someone else, there is often no need to interfere. In fact, you may cause harm if you do something. If your friends have a disagreement, discussing their differences by themselves may help them to improve their relationship. Your interference could prevent them from doing this. It may even make them feel resentful towards you. If your children have a problem, they will often learn more if they try to solve it by themselves.

In conclusion, there is no need to feel guilty if you are not always being active. Your physical and mental health will suffer if you work all the time. In addition, taking responsibility for other people's problems denies them the right to manage their own affairs. Your life will be happier and more productive if you sometimes do nothing.

Questions to think about and discuss

1   What is the thesis statement of this essay? Where has the writer placed it?
2   What are your response questions?
3   Where has the writer placed the topic sentences? Are they placed consistently?
4   Does each topic sentence help to answer the response questions *in a direct way*?
5   Has the writer used the SEX (or SEXEX) formula in every paragraph?
6   Do the topic sentences together give a clear and complete answer to the response questions?

7 Have the paragraphs been placed in a logical order? How do you think the writer decided which order to use?

8 How has the writer used transition signals to link ideas?

9 Is the introduction effective? Does it lead smoothly to the thesis statement?

10 Is the conclusion effective? How does it show the reader that the essay is finished?

11 What is your overall impression of this essay?

Sample 3: Simple expository essay

Sometimes it is all right to do nothing

In this essay, I will explain why it is sometimes all right to do nothing. Firstly, you will work better later. Secondly, your mental health will improve if you feel relaxed. In addition, you should stay at home and rest if you are sick. It is important to make sure that you have time to relax.

Doing nothing for a while will often help you to work better later. If you have been working very hard, you will be unable to work efficiently. Sitting and chatting, or just listening to music, will help you to recover more quickly. A short sleep may also be helpful. Afterwards, you will feel refreshed and will be able to concentrate again.

It may be a good idea to do nothing if you are feeling stressed. It is true that, for some people, being active helps them to forget their worries. They may be able to 'lose' themselves while playing a sport or doing some craft work. However, many people prefer to take it easy on the beach or in a peaceful park. Your mental health will improve if you feel relaxed.

Sometimes, you should do nothing if you are a little unwell. You will recover more quickly if you stay at home and rest, instead of going to work. In addition, your co-workers will not be pleased if they catch your infection. If your illness is a minor one, you might not even need to take any medication.

In conclusion, there is no need to feel guilty if you are not always being active. Your physical and mental health will suffer if you work all the time. Your life will be happier and more productive if you sometimes do nothing.

Questions to think about and discuss

1   What is the thesis statement of this essay? Where has the writer placed it?
2   What are your response questions?
3   Where has the writer placed the topic sentences? Are they placed consistently?
4   Does each topic sentence help to answer the response questions *in a direct way*?
5   Has the writer used the SEX (or SEXEX) formula in every paragraph?
6   Do the topic sentences together give a clear and complete answer to the response questions?
7   Have the paragraphs been placed in a logical order? How do you think the writer decided which order to use?
8   How has the writer used transition signals to link ideas?
9   Is the introduction effective? Does it lead smoothly to the thesis statement?
10 Is the conclusion effective? How does it show the reader that the essay is finished?
11 What is your overall impression of this essay? If you were marking it, would you give it higher or lower marks than Sample 2? Why?

Sample 4: Comparative essay

University

(Written by Kelly Li, 2003)

Recently, there has been an increase in the number of people who want to further their education by achieving a degree at university. Many of them try to study in the same way as when they were at school. However, many of them do not succeed, because they ignore an obvious fact. University is different from school.

The most significant difference is that university students' study motivations are mostly provided by themselves. Lecturers do not check students' daily homework as school teachers do. At university, each paper has a weekly study guideline. The more you have prepared, the better you can understand the lecture. If you ignore this opportunity, nobody will worry about it. In contrast, school students are more likely to depend on their teachers. This is because of the different teaching methods. Schoolteachers set homework and students who do not do their homework might be punished. Therefore, school students are regulated more than university students.

Secondly, university aims to help students develop and use researching skills much more than at school. Each university has a library which holds a wide range of books and provides electronic access to various databases. Also IT people and librarians are available to help with problems. Normally, students' assignments are based on appropriate library skills. In order to achieve good grades, students have to learn how to manage resources very well. Likewise, school also teaches students about research skills, but in a less complicated way than at university. School just gives students the basic knowledge and prepares them for a higher level of study.

Thirdly, good note-taking skills are more important at university than at school. Lecturers always talk very fast. Students not only listen to the lecturer, but also have to take notes. Sometimes it is really easy to get lost. So, using abbreviations is quite a useful strategy to speed up your note taking. However, school students have less pressure to take notes for themselves. Normally, the teacher will give handouts instead of expecting students to take notes.

Finally, the university campus is more spread out than the school. Most universities have a lot of faculties, such as business or art. Each faculty has its own building. Normally, it would not be mixed up with other faculties. Sometimes, schools combine different faculties together. So universities require larger space than school.

In summary, both university and school belong to the education system, but they treat students in different ways. Also university is more difficult than school for students to be successful. Therefore it is important to develop study skills for yourself to help with the challenges at university.

Questions to think about and discuss

1   What is the thesis statement of this essay? Where has the writer placed it?
2   What are your response questions?
3   Where has the writer placed the topic sentences? Are they placed consistently?
4   Does each topic sentence help to answer the response questions *in a direct way*?
5   Do the topic sentences together give a clear and complete answer to the response questions?
6   Has the writer used the SEX (or SEXEX) formula in every paragraph?
7   Have the paragraphs been placed in a logical order? How do you think the writer decided which order to use?
8   Has the writer used the whole picture approach or the detailed approach?
9   How has the writer used transition signals to link ideas?
10   Is the introduction effective? Does it lead smoothly to the thesis statement?
11   Is the conclusion effective? How does it show the reader that the essay is finished?
12   What is your overall impression of this essay?

Sample 5: Argumentative essay

The tongue stud debate

Body piercing has been an issue in schools for some time. In some cases, children have been suspended from school when they refused to take out their tongue studs. The schools have justified the suspensions because they said that the children did not obey the school rules. They have also said they are following the wishes of the parents. However, this attitude is misguided. Schools should be concerned about more important issues than whether a child wears a tongue stud.

Education's main concern should be to help students to learn. Schools exist to enable people to develop skills and knowledge in order to lead fulfilling and productive lives. Wearing a tongue stud does not affect a person's ability to learn. Instead of policing body piercing, schools should concentrate on providing an environment where learning is encouraged and valued.

Secondly, part of a school's responsibility is to encourage students to become law-abiding and hardworking citizens. They should learn to get on well with others and to take a full part in society. What children wear does not affect their interpersonal skills or their work habits. Therefore, schools should concentrate on their core business (education) and allow children the freedom to develop their personal identities.

Schools also have a responsibility to encourage innovative thinking. If everyone thought alike, the world would be a very boring place. New thinking is an important part of progress. Our society needs people who can question and challenge tradition, as well as people who are more conservative. Allowing adolescents the freedom to experiment encourages them to 'think outside the square'.

In this country, schools also aim to protect students' dignity and individuality. In fact, this right is supported by the Universal Declaration of Human Rights (United Nations, 1948). This means that students should be allowed to dress as they wish as long as they do not hurt others. Traditionally, the teenage years are a time for experimentation and for challenging accepted norms. At the same time, teenagers long for conformity. Their self-esteem is fragile. Harden (2002) suggests that they gain comfort in following fashion and being like their friends. Like much other body jewellery, tongue studs allow teenagers the best of both worlds: they can simultaneously shock their elders and be the same as their peers (Jetten, Branscombe, Schmitt & Spears, 2001; Whelan, 2001).

On the other hand, wearing tongue studs can be dangerous. According to O'Meara (2002), there is a risk of infection. This is because "the mouth is the dirtiest orifice in the body, bacteriologically speaking" (Carroll, 1998, p.A22). In addition, some people develop allergies to metals. A tongue stud may also damage teeth and gums. If the tongue stud breaks, the child could swallow it or choke. Active activities, especially sport, can increase the danger of this happening, so perhaps studs should be removed during sports time. However, while schools should advise students of the dangers, a total ban cannot be supported on educational grounds.

In conclusion, whether children wear tongue studs at school is not an educational concern. Instead, the schools' main focus should be on enabling children to develop appropriate skills and positive attitudes for adulthood. Wearing tongue studs is unlikely to affect children's learning and should not be an educational issue.

List of references

Carroll, P. (1998, March 18). Pierce yourself at your peril. *New Zealand Herald*, p.A22.

Harden, B. (2002, February 12). Coming to grips with the enduring appeal of body piercing. *New York Times*, p.A16.

Jetten, J., Branscombe, N.R., Schmitt, M.T., & Spears, R. (2001). Rebels with a cause: Group identification as a response to perceived discrimination from the mainstream. *Personality and Social Psychology Bulletin, 27*(9), 1204–1213.

O'Meara, S.J. (2002). Dying to get your tongue pierced? *Odyssey, 11*(15), 3.

United Nations. (1948). *Universal Declaration of Human Rights*. Retrieved May 11, 2002, from the United Nations website: http://www.un.org/Overview/rights.html

Whelan, D. (2001). Ink me, stud. *American Demographics, 23*(12), 9–11.

Questions to think about and discuss

1   In the introductory paragraph, how has the writer introduced the topic?
2   Where has the writer placed the thesis statement? Underline it.
3   What are your response question(s)?
4   Where has the writer placed the topic sentences? Do they all help to answer the response question(s) *in a direct way*?
5   Has the writer used the SEX (or SEXEX) formula in every paragraph?
6   How has the writer made each paragraph persuasive?
7   How has the writer supported his/her ideas with:
   • indirect citations?
   • direct citations?
8   Are all citations up to date?
9   How has the writer used transition signals to link ideas?
10   How has the writer constructed the concluding paragraph?
11   Check the list of references. Is it complete? Does it use Harvard or APA format? Is the format used correctly?
12   What is your overall impression of this essay?

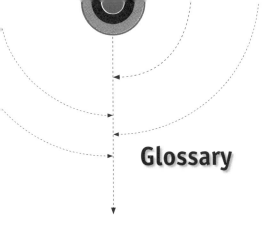

Glossary

acknowledgement A statement about where you found information or an idea.

ampersand A symbol that means "and", written &.

analyse Examine what you read and think carefully about it.

APA system A method of recording references, developed by the American Psychological Association.

argumentative essay Writing that aims to persuade the reader to agree with a point of view.

audio material Information that you listen to.

audio-visual material Information that you listen to and watch at the same time.

auditory learning style A way of understanding and remembering that involves listening.

biased Presenting only one point of view.

bibliography A list of all the sources of information that that you found about a subject.

brainstorming Thinking of as many different ideas as possible about a subject.

captive reader A person who must read a particular piece of writing.

chronological order Information is presented according to what happens first, second, third, etc.

citation A short record of a source of information that you have used in an essay; placed inside an essay.

classical structure Organisation of an argumentative essay that uses confirmation, concession and refutation.

cliché A common saying that has been used so much that it sounds boring.

clustering Deciding which information belongs together and organising it into groups.

coherent Containing information that is related.

coherent order Organisation of information so that it is logical and easy to understand.

collaborative writing Two or more people working together to produce one piece of work.

colon A symbol that separates pieces of information, written :

comparative expository essay Writing that explains two or more subjects or ideas, and identifies similarities and differences.

compound sentence A sentence with two related parts.

concession Recognition of someone else's point of view.

concise Avoiding unnecessary words so that explanations are short and concentrate on the subject.

confirmation Support for the thesis statement.

consistent spelling Using the same style of spelling, e.g. New Zealand English or Australian English or United Kingdom English or American English.

content The information and ideas that are included in an essay.

continuum A line diagram that shows how different types of something are related.

critical thinking Careful examination of something; involves thinking about how something is organised and evaluating its quality.

cyclical model A description of a flexible process in which the order of the stages can be changed or repeated.

definite article "the"; used to talk about something specific.

detailed approach An essay structure that uses each paragraph to examine a single point about two or more ideas or subjects.

direct quotation The exact words that someone has written or said.

editing The stage of the writing process when you make sure that the content is complete, relevant and well organised.

edition A reprinted version of a book, with changes from the first printing.

editor A person who organises people working together to produce a book.

electronic database A software program that contains a collection of different publications.

entertaining Making someone interested in a subject.

essay A short piece of writing that explains or discusses a point of view about a subject.

evaluate Examine something carefully and decide whether it is reliable and useful.

expository essay Writing that explains.

first draft The stage of the writing process when you use sentences to develop the outline.

free-writing Writing sentences about all the ideas you can think of.

generalisation A statement that is usually, but not always, true.

genre A category of writing that has a specific writing style.

glossary A collection of definitions of specialist vocabulary.

grammar Arrangement of words correctly, so that they make sense.

hard copy Written material that has been printed.

Harvard system A method of recording references, developed by Harvard University; sometimes called "author-date" or "name-year" system.

ICU formula Three steps for recording a reference; includes identifying the sort of publication, checking the information needed and using the correct formula.

indefinite article "a" or "an"; used for general examples.

indirect quotation A paraphrase of what someone has written or said; uses your own words.

informing Giving someone knowledge or information.

issue A subject that people have different opinions about.

issue number A number that shows when a particular journal edition was published in a year.

italics *Sloping writing.*

justify Explain the reasons for your ideas or statements.

keywords Important words about a subject.

kinaesthetic learning style A way of understanding and remembering that involves practical activity.

KISS principle Keep It Short and Simple.

learning Accepting information and ideas, and understanding and remembering them.

learning style The way that a person prefers to understand and remember information.

linear model A description of a process where several stages are completed in order.

list of references A list of the sources of information that you used in an essay.

logical order Arranged so that the reader can understand the information easily.

lower case Small letters, e.g. a, b, c.

mechanical errors Grammar, punctuation and spelling mistakes.

method A way of organising a task.

mnemonic A group of letters or words that you can use to help you remember something.

model A way of describing a process, often using words and diagrams.

oral communication Any way of finding information that involves talking or listening to people.

order of importance The most valuable idea is presented first, followed by the next most valuable idea, and so on.

outline A list of the information that will be included in an essay, and the order that it will be presented in.

overlap When different things share some of the same characteristics.

paragraph A group of sentences about one idea.

paraphrase Use your own words to explain the meaning of what someone else has written or said.

persuading Encouraging someone to accept an idea.

plagiarism Presenting other people's ideas or words as if they were your own.

planning The stage when the writer considers how to organise the essay.

proof-reading Checking that grammar, spelling and punctuation are correct.

psychological approach Organisation of information that considers the best way to convince the reader.

redundancy When words are used unnecessarily so that an idea is repeated.

referencing Recording your sources of information.

refutation (rebuttal) Statements that overcome an opposite viewpoint.

relevant About the subject that you are discussing; useful for your essay.

researching The stage of the writing process when you find information.

response question What the reader might ask after reading the thesis statement.

retrieval details Information about the database or website that you used to find a text.

reverse order of importance The weakest idea is presented first and the strongest idea last.

scan Look quickly at important parts of a text to see if it is likely to contain useful information.

search engine A software program that uses keywords to find information that has been stored electronically.

selecting Choosing.

sentence A group of words that makes sense alone and contains a complete verb.

SEX formula A way of organising a paragraph; includes statement, explanation and extra details.

simple expository essay Writing that explains one subject or idea.

skim Read very fast, reading only the important words.

soft copy Written material that is recorded electronically and has not been printed.

source Any 'place' where you find information or ideas.

spiral model A description of a process that improves a situation.

structure The way that something is organised.

target reader The person who is most likely to read a specific piece of writing.

tense A verb form that shows when something happens (or happened).

tertiary study Learning in a university or polytechnic.

text Written information.

theory and principles The 'rules' and ideas that people have developed about a particular subject.

theory of writing Specialist technical information about writing.

thesis statement A sentence that tells the reader what the essay is about and identifies the writer's point of view.

TIRC formula Think, Imagine, Record, Compare; used for paraphrasing.

topic sentence A direct answer to the response question(s); explains part or all of the thesis statement; summarises a paragraph.

transition signal A single word or a phrase that shows how information is linked (or related).

TRT formula A formula for planning an expository essay; includes thesis statement, response questions and topic sentences; helps the writer to keep on track.

truncate Shorten a keyword by deleting some letters and replacing them with a symbol; used to widen a database search.

unbiased Presenting both sides of an issue in a fair and balanced way.

unity When everything in one place belongs together.

upper case Capital letters, e.g. A, B, C.

verb A word or phrase that explains what someone or something does; or shows that someone or something exists.

verbal learning style A way of understanding and remembering that involves words, often by reading.

visual learning style A way of understanding and remembering that involves seeing information.

vocabulary The words that you use.

volume number A number that shows the year that a particular journal edition was published.

voluntary reader A person who can choose whether to read a particular piece of writing.

whole picture approach An essay structure that examines different ideas or subjects separately, then compares them.

writing The stage of the writing process when you select information and use sentences to develop the outline.

writing processes The actions that people take when they plan and complete a writing task; the order that the actions happen in.

writing style How something is written; the words that are used and the way that the information is organised.

written material Any information that contains words or pictures.

Answers to *Check your understanding* quizzes

Chapter 1

1	b	2	c
3	False	4	True
5	False	6	b
7	False	8	False
9	c	10	a

Chapter 2

1	b	2	False
3	d	4	a
5	True	6	c
7	b	8	True
9	a	10	c

Chapter 3

1	b	2	True
3	c	4	False
5	a	6	False
7	c	8	False
9	False	10	True

Chapter 4

1	a	2	False
3	True	4	c
5	True	6	c
7	False	8	b
9	False	10	b

Chapter 5

1	c	2	False
3	b	4	True
5	c	6	False
7	a	8	False
9	a	10	True

Chapter 6

1	b	2	False
3	c	4	False
5	b	6	False
7	a	8	True
9	False	10	a

Chapter 7

1	a	2	False
3	True	4	c
5	True	6	False
7	False	8	a
9	b	10	True

Chapter 8

1	c	2	True
3	b	4	b
5	a	6	True
7	False	8	b
9	False	10	True

Chapter 9

1	b	2	False
3	a	4	True
5	b	6	False
7	c	8	True
9	a	10	False

Chapter 10

1	False	2	c
3	b	4	True
5	False	6	b
7	False	8	False
9	a	10	True

Chapter 11

1	False	2	b
3	True	4	a
5	a	6	False
7	b	8	True
9	False	10	c

Chapter 12

1	False	2	b
3	True	4	d
5	False	6	b
7	False	8	True
9	True	10	a

Chapter 13

1	a	2	b
3	True	4	a
5	False	6	c
7	c	8	False
9	b	10	False

Chapter 14

1	True	2	b
3	False	4	c
5	True	6	False
7	b	8	False
9	a	10	True

Chapter 15

1	False	2	a
3	False	4	c
5	True	6	c
7	True	8	a
9	False	10	b

Chapter 16

1	b	2	False
3	True	4	d
5	False	6	c
7	True	8	True
9	False	10	a

Chapter 17

1	b	2	True
3	c	4	True
5	False	6	False
7	a	8	a
9	False	10	d

Chapter 18

1	False	2	c
3	b	4	b
5	c	6	True
7	True	8	a
9	False	10	a

Chapter 19

1	False	2	False
3	True	4	b
5	b	6	a
7	c	8	False
9	a	10	b

Chapter 20

1	b	2	False
3	a	4	False
5	False	6	False
7	c	8	b
9	False	10	c

Chapter 21

1	False	2	a
3	c	4	False
5	a	6	True
7	c	8	True
9	True	10	c

Chapter 22

1	False	2	b
3	True	4	True
5	a	6	True
7	a	8	False
9	c	10	False

Chapter 23

1	False	2	c
3	a	4	b
5	a	6	True
7	a	8	False
9	a	10	b

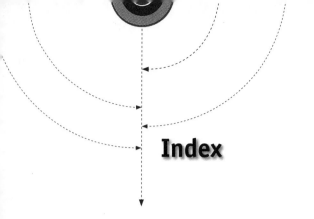

Index